GROWING OLD

YASUYUKI FUCHITA
RICHARD J. HERRING
ROBERT E. LITAN
Editors

GROWING OLD

*Paying for Retirement
and Institutional Money
Management after the
Financial Crisis*

NOMURA INSTITUTE OF CAPITAL MARKETS RESEARCH
Tokyo

BROOKINGS INSTITUTION PRESS
Washington, D.C.

Library of Congress Cataloging-in-Publication data
Growing old : paying for retirement and institutional money management after the financial
crisis / Yasuyuki Fuchita, Richard J. Herring, and Robert E. Litan, editors.
   p.   cm.
Includes bibliographical references and index.
  Summary: "Explores issues in financing retirement, from fundamental changes in types of
pension plans offered to pension funds' investment strategies following the global financial
crisis. Focuses in particular on the adequacy of individuals' and institutions' plans in the face
of increasing life expectancy and the aging of the population"—Provided by publisher.
  ISBN 978-0-8157-2153-6 (pbk. : alk. paper)
  1. Pension trusts. 2. Saving and investment. 3. Portfolio management. 4. Asset allocation.
5. Financial crises—21st century. I. Fuchita, Yasuyuki, 1958– II. Herring, Richard. III.
Litan, Robert E., 1950–IV. Title.
  HD7105.4.G76 2011
  331.25'24—dc22
                                                                2011005866

9 8 7 6 5 4 3 2 1

Printed on acid-free paper

Typeset in Adobe Garamond

Composition by Circle Graphics
Columbia, Maryland

Printed by R. R. Donnelley
Harrisonburg, Virginia

Contents

Preface   vii

1 Introduction   1
   Yasuyuki Fuchita, Richard J. Herring, and Robert E. Litan

2 Trends in Pension System Reform in East Asia:
   Japan, Korea, and China   11
   Akiko Nomura

3 The Crisis in Local Government Pensions
   in the United States   47
   Robert Novy-Marx and Joshua Rauh

4 Managing Risks in Defined Contribution Plans:
   What Does the Future Hold?   75
   Olivia S. Mitchell

5 Asset Allocation by Institutional Investors
   after the Recent Financial Crisis   95
   Robert C. Pozen, Betsy Palmer, and Natalie Shapiro

Contributors   143

Index   145

Preface

IN 2004 THE Brookings Institution joined with Nomura Institute of Capital Markets Research to showcase research on selected topics in financial market structure and regulation of interest to policymakers, scholars, and market practitioners in the United States, Japan, and elsewhere. Initially led by Brookings senior fellow Robert E. Litan and Yasuyuki Fuchita, senior managing director of Nomura Institute of Capital Markets Research, the collaboration was joined in 2008 by Richard J. Herring of the Financial Institutions Center at the Wharton School of the University of Pennsylvania. The collaboration has convened a conference each year since 2004, leading to five volumes published by Brookings Institution Press, the most recent entitled *After the Crash: The Future of Finance* (2010).

The chapters in this sixth volume in the series are based on presentations made at the conference "Growing Old: Paying for Retirement and Institutional Money Management after the Financial Crisis," held on October 15, 2010, at the Brookings Institution in Washington, D.C. The conference considered the future of the financial services industry after the crisis of 2007–2008 and focused on commercial banks, investment banks, and hedge funds in particular. All of the chapters represent the views of the authors and not necessarily those of the staff, officers, or trustees of the Brookings Institution, the Nomura Institute of Capital Markets Research, or the Wharton Financial Institutions Center.

The editors thank Matthew Garza for outstanding research assistance and for checking the factual accuracy of the manuscript; Eileen Hughes for careful editing; and Lindsey Wilson for organizing the conference and providing administrative assistance. Both the conference and this publication were funded in part by Nomura Foundation.

YASUYUKI FUCHITA
RICHARD J. HERRING
ROBERT E. LITAN

1

Introduction

T HE RECENT FINANCIAL CRISIS and subsequent recession resulted from a series of major failings: excessive incentives for lenders to originate subprime mortgages and for others to securitize them; poor risk management by financial institutions; serious failures of oversight by state and federal financial regulators; and far too much leverage in too many financial institutions and households. While the immediate dangers from the crisis have abated—the financial system has returned to profitability and the economy is growing, albeit slowly—the damage to the economy will linger for years.

Among the many impacts of the crisis is the growing interest in early retirement, perhaps because so many of the older unemployed are unlikely to find another job. That, in turn, has highlighted a problem that may be most acute in the United States: how government and private companies will honor their obligations under "defined benefit" (DB) pension plans—those that promise a post-retirement stream of payments based on some combination of workers' seniority, their average or highest level of pay, and perhaps other factors. The yawning gap between the costs to support pension obligations and the funds available to cover the costs is, without overstatement, highly disturbing if not alarming. In part the problem is one of demographics: the number of workers relative to the number of retirees has been shrinking and will continue to do so. But that challenge has long been

The authors wish to thank Matthew Garza for his extraordinary assistance in preparing this chapter.

I

known and therefore cannot fully explain the shortfalls. Why, then, are so many pension schemes so hard pressed?

One widely publicized answer lies in the generosity of many plans. The anecdotes are many. In California, for example, more than 9,000 state and local managers have retirement incomes of over $100,000 a year. Public schemes often calculate benefits based on final salary rather than average salary and allow employees to cash out unused sick days without limit. Private companies have been shying away from such commitments for some time now, but the original plans still exist and the residual commitments are significant. Although most pension plans in the United States today are "defined contribution" (DC) plans—which are based on a worker's own contributions, typically with some employer match—as of 2006, DB plans could still be found in two-thirds of the companies in the S&P 500.

A second answer lies in the tangle of accounting standards and actuarial conventions that allow DB plan sponsors, especially those in the public sector, to obscure the extent of their obligations and to scrimp on funding. To be sure, calculating those obligations is complicated, but current rules often permit generous return estimates of 8 percent while eschewing best practice techniques such as risk adjusting expected returns. That is especially pertinent because regardless of financial performance, pension fund obligations will need to be paid. With market returns on risk-free or low-risk assets having been driven to record low levels by the Fed and other monetary authorities, how will or can these obligations be met? That question vexes not only pension funds, but insurance companies, university and charitable endowments, and other institutional investors.

Questions regarding the future of pension plans and institutional investment following the financial crisis were the centerpiece of the 2010 conference on financial policy issues jointly organized by the Nomura Institute of Capital Markets Research, the Brookings Institution, and the Wharton Financial Institutions Center and held at Brookings in October 2010. This volume contains revised versions of four papers presented at the conference.

This introductory chapter provides a summary of the chapters that follow. The broad theme that runs throughout the chapters is that DB pension systems are in direct need of reform and that there exists no better time than the present to reckon with the challenges involved.

Akiko Nomura, of the Nomura Institute of Capital Markets Research, contextualizes the global nature of pension reform in chapter 2 by examining what has been happening in Japan, Korea, and China. The discussion in this chapter provides a useful introduction to many issues that relate to the United States and Western Europe as well, which are addressed in the remaining chapters.

Nomura identifies three global trends in pension reform: a shift from public to private pensions, increased levels of prefunding, and a shift from DB to DC plans. She finds that the three countries that she examines in detail are broadly following the global trends but with particular and important deviations.

The three countries—Japan, Korea, and China—were not by chosen by accident. They are the subject of analysis because of both their global prominence and their diversity relative to one another. Japan is a country of 127 million people; Korea, 48 million; and China, 1.3 billion. Their histories with pensions are similarly varied. Japan began a public scheme as far back as 1942, whereas Korea and China launched their public programs much more recently, in 1988 and 1990, respectively. Japanese corporate pension plans also are by far the oldest, dating back some fifty years; corporate launches took place only in 2004 for China and 2005 for Korea. For all the differences in their program history and design, however, each country faces the same demographic challenge: the share of the population aged sixty-five and older is growing, meaning that a larger base of beneficiaries must be supported by a relatively smaller base of workers. While Japan's issues with a shrinking and aging population are well known, Korea and even populous China must grapple with the aging of their populations. How these countries are attempting to deal with this challenge is instructive.

A pension scheme that functions well will be both sustainable and adequate. That is, its funding will be secure and it will provide a respectable standard of living. While both of those goals are necessary, each places tension on the other. As budget pressures grow, steps must be taken to reduce that tension. For example, replacement rates—the percentage of a worker's salary that a pension provides in retirement—are a good measure of adequacy. Given mounting budget pressures, those rates are being lowered in both Japan and Korea, to 50 percent and 40 percent, respectively—both lower than the OECD average of 59 percent. In addition, both Korea and Japan are raising their plan premiums (contributions). The cumulative effect of the reforms is to weaken the role of public pensions in supporting people in their retirement years: people are being asked to pay more for less. That obviously increases demand for private retirement plans.

But how meaningful have private pension plans been to date? Nomura explores that issue by comparing estimates of private pension assets as a percentage of GDP. The OECD average is 74.5 percent, and all three countries come in well below that rate: looking at corporate pension assets, the percentages are 12 percent in Japan, 8 percent in Korea, and 1 percent in China. Of course, the relative youth of those schemes accounts for their relatively low share of GDP, but that is only a partial explanation. Weak coverage also is a major component. In Korea, only 13 percent of companies even offer a pension plan and coverage hovers at around 22 percent of workers; in Japan, less than half of workers are covered; and in China, only about 1 percent are covered (even the coverage of China's public system is low, at 20 percent of the population). So, while private schemes are being asked to make up for shrinking public offerings, they have a long way to go before they will fill the gaps.

Another important trend in the pension systems that Nomura reviews relates to the way that the massive public pension reserves that arise from prefunding are being handled. For example, Japan's Government Pension Investment Fund is the world's largest, at $1.3 trillion, more than triple the next-largest fund. Korea oversees $235 billion, and China's prefunding reserve is at $114 billion. Nomura observes that however substantial, those funds are not being governed in a manner consistent with international best practice. The funds in China and Korea are overseen by a board of directors, but the boards are stacked with government officials. The chairman of Korea's board is also the minister of health, welfare, and family affairs. China's board includes several vice ministers. Japan's reserve fund does not even have a governing body; the bulk of all decisionmaking, including asset selection, is vested in one person. Clearly, there is much to improve in the governance of these pension reserve funds.

Nomura concludes by discussing the growing importance of DC plans in the three countries. Of the group, China is moving most aggressively toward DC systems. Indeed, its public pension scheme has a funded DC component, and newly introduced corporate pension schemes are to offer only DC plans. In Japan and Korea, DC plans have been introduced but have not yet grown to their full potential. However, changes such as the introduction of new accounting rules that mandate recognition of pension obligations on financial statements without smoothing adjustments are spurring further interest in DC plans.

The rise of DC plans has left all three countries wrestling with how to guide workers in making their investment decisions. China does not allow DC plan participants to direct any of their own monies. Instead, a designated trustee, whether a corporate pension board or a trust investment company, is responsible for investment decisions. For corporate pension schemes, Korea has asset allocation limits and bans investment in individual stocks, equity funds, or balanced funds. Japan mandates the offering of at least one "principal secured" product in DC plans.

Nomura believes that embracing DC plans is the only way to allow private schemes to make up for the shrinking role of public pensions. It remains to be seen how the three countries that she reviews will succeed in this regard; East Asia may yet provide models for the rest of the world in managing pension schemes, but that possibility is not yet a reality.

In chapter 3 Robert Novy-Marx and Joshua Rauh address an issue that has received growing attention in the United States, largely because of their own past work: how large are municipal pension obligations in the United States? One would think that producing an answer would be a straightforward proposition: make a few phone calls, download the spreadsheets, and then add up the amounts. The reality is much different and much more difficult. For one thing, reporting and disclosure by municipalities about any and all of their obligations is far from uniform. Yet even if that problem did not exist, the current accounting framework for measuring pension obligations grossly understates the amount that local governments owe.

First, what do municipalities estimate their pension liabilities to be? Using data that include approximately two-thirds of local government employees, the authors calculate that the total amount of unfunded liabilities reported by all major municipalities is $190 billion. However, taking account of what they estimate to be the entire universe of all municipal employers, they provide a more realistic figure for unfunded liabilities: $574 billion, roughly triple the reported estimate.

What accounts for the stark difference in numbers? Perhaps the most significant factor concerns the "discount rate," the rate at which liabilities far in the future—often as long as twenty to thirty years—must be reduced to bring them to their present value. That must be done because a dollar today is worth more than a dollar to be paid in the future, since the dollar now can be reinvested at a given rate of interest—the discount rate—to realize a larger sum in the future. By the same reasoning, one needs less than a dollar today to pay off a dollar of obligation in the future. The more distant the time in the future that liability must be paid, the smaller the discounted present value of the liability.

A main problem with the current reporting of municipal pension obligations is that the interest or discount rate used to discount future liabilities back to the present—an assumed return on assets of 8 percent—looks far too high in the current low-interest environment. A more realistic, lower discount rate means that it takes more dollars today to pay off future dollar obligations because the investment earns a lower interest rate in the meantime. Accordingly, the use of an unrealistically high discount rate of 8 percent translates into unrealistically *low* estimates for the present value of future pension obligations.

To realize the assumed 8 percent rate of return, municipalities are driven to invest in riskier assets—for example, by moving high-quality debt to junk bonds. The authors offer a metaphor to highlight the shortcoming here. Imagine an individual writing down the value of her mortgage simply by shifting savings from a money market account to the stock market. It is convenient accounting, but does not alter the reality of the situation.

Novy-Marx and Rauh examine two alternative possibilities for discount rates to measure pension liabilities: those implied by yield curves (a graph of interest rates by length of maturity of the obligation) of taxable AA+ municipal bonds and Treasury bonds. The first method treats pension obligations as what they are—debts—and accordingly uses the cost of municipal borrowing as the discount rate. However, it is possible to argue that pensioners have greater rights even than bondholders, in which case the most appropriate discount rate would be the interest that they could earn as asset holders—the "risk free" Treasury yield. This "risk free" rate is what the authors use to arrive at the figure quotes above.

In fact, the legal rights of pensioners are ambiguous, and they are the subject of litigation around the country. Government efforts to tinker with cost-of-living benefit adjustments in Colorado and Minnesota already have resulted in court battles. Some states even have pension protection made explicit in their constitutions. So while municipalities, unlike states, can declare bankruptcy, it is not clear if that would do anything to change their pension obligations.

There is an additional reason that the current reported municipal pension obligations are understated. The authors' (and the municipalities') calculations are based on accumulated benefit obligations (ABO), a number that measures only liabilities accrued to date, thereby excluding the growth of obligations as employees continue to work and earn benefits. So if municipalities were to engage in a (hypothetical) hard freeze of all further pension benefits, the ABO numbers would not shrink but only cease growing. Even so, many municipalities already are headed for trouble. Even assuming an 8 percent return on existing assets, they allow for current assets and future returns to fund ABO obligations (those already accrued to date). In this exercise, six municipalities will have run out of money by 2020: Boston, Chicago, Cincinnati, Jacksonville, Philadelphia, and St. Paul. An additional thirty-six will have failed by 2030.

The point is not that collapse is imminent, but rather that the current track is unsustainable. Growing pension liabilities have the potential to crowd out other government services, and they may portend higher taxes. It is apparent that governments cannot continue to ignore their own fiscal situation any longer. What direction reforms will take remains to be seen.

Given all that has been said here up to this point about DB pension plans, which will be discussed in much greater detail in chapters 2 and 3, it is not surprising that many plan sponsors have been turning to DC plans instead. DC plans certainly have attractive features: they are portable, transparent, and cannot fail to deliver on their promises, for they make none. But DC plans gain those advantages by shifting the risks of pension plan performance from sponsors to employee participants. What exactly is the nature of those risks, to both the individual and the larger society? What can be done to mitigate the risks? And, more important, is the DC design up to the task of ensuring a stable and comfortable retirement for plan participants? Olivia Mitchell takes up these matters in chapter 4.

The recent financial crisis underscores the need to acknowledge the danger of pension asset exposure to the markets. Pension funds, just like other funds, are susceptible to market volatility. In 2008, for example, U.S. pension assets fell by an eye-popping 20 percent, a drop that unfortunately coincided with the beginning of the retirement of baby boomers. Globally, the fallout was similar for a broad range of OECD countries. Not all of that money was invested in DC plans, but the point still holds: pension assets, like any other portfolio of assets, are vulnerable.

Mitchell identifies four particular types of risk that exist in the design of DC plans: individual risk, institutional risk, country risk, and global risk. In an ideal world (one in which what economic theory predicts should happen does happen), saving and investing during an individual's younger years provides a base of support for the individual during retirement. While this model accurately describes the profile of an average individual, across the population many people will deviate from the model. They may be out of work or in debt and therefore unable to save (or to dip into savings during hard times). Or—and this failing is all too common—they may not be aware of how expensive retirement will be.

For example, in surveys of baby boomers across the United States, Mitchell found that significant percentages of them could not perform basic division (43 percent) or demonstrate an understanding of compound interest (82 percent). Those individuals already have a lifetime of financial decisions behind them, so those percentages are cause for concern, especially since financial literacy is a strong predictor of successfully planning for retirement. While some employers do support DC participants with financial seminars and easy-to-use financial planning calculators, basic gaps in knowledge will need to be addressed. Automatic enrollment (or opt-out plans) and life-cycle funds are possible solutions to these problems.

Where else is risk present? People are living much longer now than before. That is a welcome trend, but planning for a retirement that may span decades only adds to the difficulty. By definition half of the members of the population will outlive their life expectancy, and that raises the possibility of retirees outliving their savings. In a DC plan that risk is amplified since most plans do not offer the option of an in-plan payout annuity. While retirees may withdraw their money in phases or purchase lifetime payout annuities, few actually do so.

Risk can also be found in the national and global arenas, both of which are highly unpredictable. On the national front, government budgets are a major issue: expected payments from government programs may be reduced in the future as governments try to rein in deficits. In addition, the potential insolvency of private sector pension plans is at issue. On the global front, the recent crisis demonstrates that when asset prices in global markets are highly correlated, there are few if any safe havens. Risk cannot always be diversified away.

What can be done about these challenges? Mitchell discusses a few potential solutions. Financial education is one prominent idea; people need to understand the risks before they can begin to mitigate them.[1] Even with a lot of education, though, complete (naked) exposure to the markets in DC plans might not be appropriate for many people. Embedding some kind of payment guarantee in the plans could be helpful, but that would inevitably raise premiums. Other ideas include automatically enrolling participants in target maturity date funds, requiring the purchase of annuities, and creating new financial products for an aging population (such as long-term care insurance or mortality securitization).

Recognizing the new pension landscape facing DC plan participants along with its attendant risks is critical. The DC scheme has yet to be proven successful at securing the retirement income of the broader population, and the new environment will demand considerable attention and innovative solutions.

While many DC plan participants may be unaware of their own market position or lack a coherent and long-term plan to save for retirement, the same cannot be said for institutional investors who manage major funds for foundations, university endowments, and pension plans. Nevertheless, professional investors were no less immune to the recent market turmoil. Bob Pozen, Betsy Palmer, and Natalie Shapiro examine issues related to such investors in chapter 5. They look specifically at the asset allocation—the division of an institution's capital among a variety of asset classes, such as stocks or bonds—of institutional investors in the wake of the financial crisis. The authors note that over 80 percent of long-term performance is determined by broad asset allocation decisions, so clearly asset allocation is critical.

The authors identify three main trends that they believe emerged during the rocky period from 2007 to 2009. First, the allocation to equities in general declined, although there was a shift from domestic equities to international stocks. Second, there was an increase in allocations to fixed-income securities. And third, there also was an increase in allocations to alternative investments.

---

1. To that end, Mitchell and some collaborators invented a video game to help younger generations learn about finance. See Financial Entertainment, "Celebrity Calamity" (http://financialentertainment.org/play/celebritycalamity.html).

With global stocks having fallen by 50 percent in 2008, the move away from stocks during that period was not surprising, but the magnitude of the shift is still significant. Institutional investors in the United States decreased their allocation to equities from 47 percent in 2005 to 32 percent in 2009. The trend was similar in the United Kingdom and Japan.

The extent of the equity reallocations depends on the risk preferences and market outlook of various investors. Some make an argument in favor of international positions for diversification, but others, notably corporate DB plans, perceive more risk in international arenas. Removing risk is important to all these investors. That helps to explain the rising importance of fixed-income investments, particularly domestic fixed-income investments. State and local government funds increased their allocation to such investments by 19 percent and U.S. corporations by 85 percent. The exception has been European institutional investors who, given fixed-income allocations roughly three times as large as those in the United States, decreased their bond holdings from 61 to 55 percent.

The irony of the movement out of equities and into fixed income is that many institutional investors, notably pension funds, need high returns to fill their funding deficits. The market upheaval that took place during the crisis left these investors scrambling for a safe haven, but the returns on fixed income are too small to meet larger fund goals. Moreover, the market rebound in the wake of crisis was considerable—in the twelve months that ended March 21, 2010, the S&P 500 index increased by roughly 50 percent. The uptick in interest in fixed-income investments after the crash thus may have been short-sighted.

Finally there is the growing allocation to alternative investments such as private equity, hedge funds, and real estate. Historically, U.S. endowments and foundations have had the greatest interest in private equity, but recent survey results suggest broader interest. Globally, more than 10 percent of investors expressed their intent to "significantly increase" their allocations to private equity. Investors in Asia (excluding Japan) were by far the most enthusiastic—fully half of investors surveyed indicated their desire to ramp up their investments. The trends for hedge funds and real estate are broadly similar: growing interest in the asset class and an appetite among a core group of investors to "significantly increase" their holdings.

Given that holdings of alternative assets typically have been small, there is room for considerable growth. Whether returns from alternative investments have the same growth potential is another matter. Public pensions are especially high on alternative assets, putting a large burden on them to perform well; if they do not, pensions may face some hard choices down the road, such as whether to reduce benefits and/or raise contributions. However, alternative assets have not always produced positive returns, and returns across managers vary. The authors playfully mention Lake Wobegon, the mythical town where all children are above average. The same belief in private equity and hedge funds may leave many institutions sorely disappointed.

An honest reckoning with the task of paying for an aging population is disheartening. Government budgets are under strain, personal savings are meager, and the markets will not spare us hard choices in the near future. But despair need not be the takeaway from this research. As noted above, the financial crisis has forced us to consider lots of hard questions, and we hope that one contribution of the conference and this volume will be to provide an initial round of answers. The chapters that follow document the extent of the problem and outline what trade-offs we face going forward. That is a first step. The challenge now is to dig deeper and ultimately take action.

AKIKO NOMURA

2

Trends in Pension System Reform in East Asia: Japan, Korea, and China

A NUMBER OF DEVELOPED COUNTRIES have been reforming their pension systems to adapt to their aging populations. Three trends in those reforms can be briefly summarized as a shift from public to private pensions, an increase in the level of prefunding, and a shift from defined benefit plans to defined contribution plans, all aimed at improving both the adequacy and sustainability of pensions.

The pension reforms under way in three East Asian countries—Japan, Korea, and the People's Republic of China—seem to be following basically the same path. A closer look at the details, however, indicates that each country has its own set of issues and fairly large differences with the overall trends in some areas.

Both Japan and Korea have been lowering the replacement rate of their public pensions. Korea is incrementally lowering its replacement rate from 70 percent to 40 percent, and it also introduced a corporate pension system.[1] Japan too has already passed revisions that will bring its replacement rate down to 50 percent from 59 percent.[2] However, the coverage rate of Japan's corporate pensions is actually in a declining trend. While Korea is still at the stage of observing how the newly introduced corporate pension plans fare, more focus should be put on policy measures to expand private pensions in Japan.

1. Park (2009, p.44).
2. Japan Ministry of Health, Labor, and Welfare (2005).

Japan, Korea, and China have made some achievements in public pension prefunding. China has introduced funded personal accounts as a component of its public pension. Japan's Government Pension Investment Fund (GPIF) is the largest pension fund in the world, while Korea's National Pension Fund (NPF) and China's National Social Security Fund (NSSF) have also built up sizable assets. All three countries, however, have room for improving the governance of the organizations that manage their reserve funds.

China is taking an aggressive approach in the shift from defined benefit to defined contribution plans with its mandate that all new corporate pensions must be of the latter type. In Japan and Korea, both defined benefit plans and defined contribution plans are offered. Measures to strengthen the latter are needed to make corporate pensions more sustainable in Japan.

Underlying Trends in Pension Reform

The roles and objectives of pension systems differ from country to country, but one objective common to all is to provide a degree of old age income security to a wide range of the population. The limits to achieving that objective by using market principles and self-help efforts alone have justified state involvement in pension systems. State involvement includes the establishment of public pension programs as well as government policies that support corporate, occupational, and other private pensions.

Population aging is probably the single factor with the greatest impact on pension systems worldwide. In the short run, the pressure that pension benefits put on national treasuries often sparks debate over pension reform. If pension costs were completely paid for with insurance premiums and received no funding from general revenue, national treasuries would not be directly affected. However, because many public pensions are supported by taxes and used as a tool to redistribute income, during times like the present, when fiscal deficits are growing rapidly, attention is naturally drawn to the cost of social security benefits, which is a mandatory budget expenditure. In addition, tax relief on private pensions must be paid for, and normally the need for relief also comes under closer scrutiny when fiscal deficits are growing. Over the longer term, however, it is population aging that creates the greatest pressure for pension reform, primarily because the most widely used method of financing public pensions is pay-as-you-go (PAYGO) financing. When the population ages faster than expected, it destroys the balance between the working generations and the retired generations, which in turn causes pension finances to deteriorate.

Since the 1990s, many countries, primarily those with more advanced economies, have instituted various pension reforms to adapt to the aging of their populations. The objective of the reforms has been to make pensions both more sustainable and more adequate. "More sustainable" means "more affordable" from the perspective of individuals, employers, and the national treasury, and it means "more financially sound" from the perspective of pension finances. Achieving that objective means making the pension system more robust to future demographic changes. Ensuring the adequacy of pensions means ensuring that a broader slice of the population participates in a pension plan (a higher coverage rate) and receives a reasonable level of retirement income.

The underlying theme of recent pension reforms in the developed countries can be briefly summarized as a shift from public to private pensions, an increase in prefunding, and a shift from defined benefit plans to defined contribution plans or some combination of the three. The first trend, the shift from public to private pensions, may be inevitable, given that as populations become older, public pensions are bound to play a reduced role to ensure greater sustainability of pensions. People draw on both public and private pensions to ensure that they have the funds that they need for old age, but the question of how the burden is to be shared by the two systems remains. Specifically, how much should the government assist people in their own efforts to ensure retirement income above the minimum benefit, and to what extent should the government pursue policies to strengthen private pensions?

Generally, public pensions are PAYGO and private pensions are prefunded. A shift to private pensions therefore means greater prefunding, although recently there has been more focus on establishing and managing public pension reserve funds. Putting greater emphasis on prefunding can lessen the impact that societal aging has on pension finances and make pensions more sustainable.

The shift from defined benefit to defined contribution plans is occurring to varying degrees in most developed countries, mainly in workplace pensions, including corporate pensions. It has become more difficult for employers to offer defined benefit plans, which obligate them to make contributions and absorb the investment risk in order to ensure that the promised benefits can be paid. Consequently, defined contribution plans are becoming the plans of choice. Some public pensions also are shifting from a defined benefit to a defined contribution structure. One example is the notional defined contribution plan. Although it is a PAYGO system, it provides greater clarity regarding the relationship between contributions and benefits. Another example is either the partial or full implementation of a funded defined contribution plan for public pensions.

The Asian countries that currently are the nexus of global growth are expected to experience population aging over the long term, albeit to differing degrees and

Figure 2-1. *Percent of the Population Aged 65 and Older, Selected Countries*

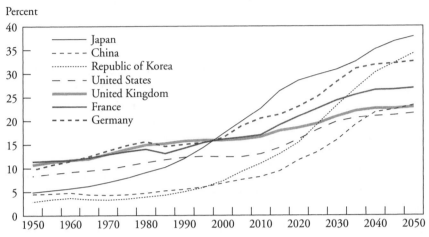

Percent

Source: United Nations (2009).

on differing time horizons. The level of both economic and social development varies widely across Asia, and the same is true of national pension systems. The focus in this chapter is on three countries—Japan, Korea, and China—that provide an interesting combination of population, economic size, extent of population aging (figure 2-1), types of pensions, and presence of reserve funds. Japan, one of the most mature economies in the world, faces a serious pension problem as a result of the rate at which its population has been aging. Korea is classified as a developed country, like Japan, but its pension system is relatively new. China differs considerably in terms of its stage of economic development and social structure, but the workability of its pension system attracts considerable attention because of the sheer size of its population and its great importance to the global economy.

This chapter provides a brief overview of the systems being used in Japan, Korea, and China and then looks more closely at the shift from public to private pensions, at increased prefunding, and at the shift from defined benefit to defined contribution plans in these three countries.

Overview of Pension Schemes in Three East Asian Countries

In many countries, people have access to multiple types of pensions, both public and private. The conceptual framework for pension systems drawn up by the World Bank also is based on the thinking that providing multiple pension types makes it possible to build a system that reaches a more diverse range of groups within a population.[3]

The World Bank's framework categorizes pensions into multiple pillars, from 0 to 4. The conceptual framework published in 1994 defined the first pillar as mandatory, PAYGO, defined benefit public pensions; the second pillar as mandatory, funded, defined contribution private pensions; and the third pillar as voluntary savings for retirement. A zero pillar and a fourth pillar were added in the conceptual framework published in 2005.[4] The zero pillar guarantees a minimum pension funded by tax revenue. The first pillar is based on mandatory enrollment and payment of social insurance premiums by the working-age population. The level of the premium is based on income, and the pension benefit provided is meant to replace that income to a certain extent. The second pillar is a system of mandatory private accounts. The third pillar, which is voluntary, can take various forms, including workplace-based or individual-based accounts and defined benefit or defined contribution plans. The fourth pillar consists of informal family support of and intergenerational wealth transfers to the elderly.

Table 2-1 looks at the pension systems in Japan, Korea, and China within the context of the World Bank's conceptual framework. All three countries take a multi-pillar approach to pensions.

Japan's Pension Schemes

Japan's public pension has two tiers, a fixed basic pension benefit paid to all citizens and an earnings-related benefit for private sector employees and government employees. On top of these are private pension plans, including both defined benefit and defined contribution plans.

Private sector employees and government employees enroll in the public pension through their workplace, with the earnings-related premium (contribution) split between the employer and employee. The benefits received are a combination of the basic pension and the earnings-related pension. The system for private sector employees is Employees' Pension Insurance (EPI), and the system for government employees is called the Mutual Aid Pension. Employees' spouses who have no income do not directly pay a premium, but they receive a basic pension. The self-employed join the National Pension Insurance (NPI), pay a fixed premium, and receive a basic pension. The basic pension serves as a common ground for all people.

---

3. Holzmann and Hinz (2005).
4. Holzmann and Hinz (2005, p. 42).

Table 2-1. *Description of the Pension Systems in Japan, Korea, and China, within the World Bank Framework*

World Bank framework	*Overview*	*Japan*	*Korea*	*China*
Zero pillar: Social security funded by taxes	Basic pension, universal pension with means testing. Targeted enrollment: those missed by the universal pension or other system. Funding source: general revenue.	One-half of the cost of basic pension benefits is funded by general revenue.	Basic old age pension with means testing.	None.
First pillar: Public pension with mandatory enrollment	Public pension, defined benefit/notional defined contribution. Targeted enrollment: mandatory enrollees. Funding source: premiums and pension reserves.	There are two tiers: a basic pension for all people and a system for employees. Separate systems are established for the self-employed, private sector employees, and government employees.	National pension and public employee pension.	Basic endowment insurance.

Second pillar: Private pension with mandatory enrollment	Occupational pensions/individual pensions, funded defined benefit and defined contribution plans. Targeted enrollment: mandatory enrollees. Funding source: financial assets.	None.	Employers are required to provide retirement pay system or retirement pension plan.	None.
Third pillar: Voluntary private pension	Occupational pensions/individual pensions, funded defined benefit and defined contribution plans. Targeted enrollment: voluntary enrollees. Funding source: financial assets.	Defined benefit pension. Defined contribution pension (corporate/individual).	Pensions include both defined benefit and defined contribution plans.	New corporate pensions are DC plans.
Fourth pillar: Nonfinancial support	Access to other formal programs (health care) as well as informal programs, such as family support, and other individual financial and nonfinancial assets. Targeted enrollment: voluntary enrollees. Funding source: Financial and nonfinancial assets.	Yes.	Yes.	Yes.

Source: Developed by Nomura Institute of Capital Markets Research based on information on each country's pension system.

Japan has two types of private pensions, defined benefit and defined contribution. There are three defined benefit (DB) plans available, the Employees' Pension Fund (EPF), DB corporate pension (DBCP) plans, and tax-qualified pension plans (TQPPs). The 2001 corporate pension reforms included legislation to phase out TQPPs by March 2012 and introduce DBCP plans. DC pension plans also were introduced in the 2001 reforms. DC plans include corporate DC plans offered by companies to their employees and personal DC plans for the self-employed and employees of companies without a corporate pension.

Korea's Pension Schemes

Korea's pension system comprises a public pension launched in 1988 and corporate pensions begun in 2005. Enrollment in the public pension is mandatory for employees, who enroll through the workplace, and for the self-employed, who enroll in individual plans, but it is voluntary for spouses without an income. Premiums, which are set at 9 percent of income, are split between the employer and employee for workplace enrollees and paid entirely by individual enrollees.

The benefit from the basic pension is determined by the number of years that participants have paid into the system and their average income over that entire period, as well as by the average income of all mandatory participants over their last three years prior to retirement. The inclusion of the latter gives the system an element of income redistribution.

Korea is unique in that companies are required to provide employees a pension plan or a lump-sum retirement pay system. The retirement pay system began as a voluntary system in 1953, but companies became obligated to offer it in 1961, which resulted in its widespread adoption. However, apparently there were problems in ensuring participants' benefits since the system was in book reserve form, and the government responded by introducing employee retirement reserve insurance, retirement insurance, and retirement trusts to encourage saving outside the company.[5] There were a number of problems with those options as well, including that companies were able to use their employees' retirement reserve insurance as collateral to borrow money and that there was no mechanism for verifying the funding of retirement insurance and retirement trusts.

Korea introduced corporate pensions in 2005 with the passage of the Employee Retirement Benefit Security Act. Two types of such pensions are offered, defined benefit and defined contribution. Individual retirement accounts (IRAs) also were introduced to ensure portability when employees change jobs.

5. Ryu (2010).

In step with that, the government decided to abolish employee retirement reserve insurance, retirement insurance, and retirement trusts.

China's Pension Schemes

Enrollment in basic endowment insurance, China's public pension system, is mandatory. The system comprises employees and the self-employed in urban areas. In China, state-owned enterprises used to provide the social safety net, but the system has been reformed several times since the 1990s, resulting in the current combination of a public pension (basic endowment insurance) and voluntary corporate pensions.[6]

Basic endowment insurance is two tiered. The first tier is a common pool, and the second is individual accounts. Employers contribute a premium set at 20 percent of total wages paid to the common pool, and employees contribute 8 percent of their average wage to their individual account. The common pool is a PAYGO defined benefit pension, while the individual accounts are a funded, defined contribution pension. This mix of PAYGO with a funded, defined contribution pension is also used by Sweden for its public pension. Unlike in Sweden, however, participants in China's basic endowment insurance cannot decide how to invest the funds in their individual accounts, which are basically invested in government bonds through the basic endowment insurance fund.

The corporate pension system that China introduced in 2004 is noteworthy in that it is offered only as a DC plan. Companies can decide whether to offer a corporate pension or not, and both the company and the employee make contributions.

The Shift from Public to Private Pensions

Although there appears to be a trade-off between making pensions more sustainable and ensuring their adequacy, in reality both must be achieved at the same time for reforms to work well. If benefits are continued without regard to sustainability while the population ages, financial realities will eventually force reductions in benefits, thereby adversely affecting their adequacy. Likewise, if pension benefits are too low, confidence in the system itself is undermined, opening the way to undisciplined political pressure that raises benefits, thereby adversely affecting their sustainability. Ultimately, each country must find its own optimal balance of the two.

---

6. This section draws heavily on Sekine (2009).

Table 2-2. *Replacement Rate of Public Pensions*

Japan	The 2004 reform lowered the replacement rate from about 59 percent to just over 50 percent, based on the model household (single-earner couple household with two children, forty years' enrollment). According to the OECD, the gross replacement rate following the reforms will be 33.9 percent.
Korea	The 2007 reform lowered the replacement rate from 60 percent in 2008 to 50 percent and then lowered it further in 0.5 percentage point increments until it reaches 40 percent in 2028. According to the OECD, the gross replacement rate following the reforms will be 42.1 percent.
China	The OECD estimates the replacement rate to be 35 percent for the socially pooled account and 24.2 percent for the individual accounts, for a total of 59.2 percent.
OECD average	The average replacement rate for OECD countries in 2009 for public pensions and mandatory private pensions combined was 59.0 percent; the rate for public pensions only was 45.7 percent.

Source: Nomura Institute of Capital Markets Research, based on OECD (2009).

One of the primary indicators of the adequacy of pension benefits is their replacement rate. Many European countries began lowering the replacement rate of their public pensions in the 1990s: Germany, from 48.7 to 39.9 percent, and France, from 64.7 to 51.2 percent, for example.[7] As discussed below, Japan and Korea have adopted similar measures (table 2-2).

The Role of Public Pensions Is Bound to Shrink in Japan and Korea

Japan's Employees' Pension Insurance had long used a graduated premium approach to funding, and therefore future premium hikes had been taken as a given. The funding mechanism was designed from the outset to incorporate future incremental increases in the premium rate, and the current rate was based on future expected increases. Because costs were postponed under that funding method, it created a larger financial burden for future generations.

Public pension reform in 2004 put an end to that method, gradually raising premiums to deal with the problem of underfunded pension benefits. At the same time, in order to limit the burden on the working generation, the 2004 reform fixed the premium after increases at ¥16,900 ($205) for National Pension Insurance

7. OECD (2007, p. 66).

and 18.3 percent for the EPI, and it also established a schedule for adjusting benefit levels to accommodate the impact of demographics.[8] More specifically, an automatic adjustment of benefits based on demographics ("macroeconomic slide") is accompanied by a lowering of the replacement rate for the model household to 50 percent from 59 percent.[9] In addition, the share of the basic pension benefit funded by general tax revenues was raised from one-third to one-half.

In general, an increase in funding from general taxes means strengthening the security of the minimum benefit by redistributing income to the lower-income classes. Japan's 2004 reforms did not, however, clearly position the basic pension as a minimum benefit. One of the policy issues championed by the Democratic Party of Japan (DPJ), which took power in September 2009, was public pension reform. The DPJ proposed a major reform that would combine an income-related pension plan in which everyone participated, including employees and the self-employed, and a minimum benefit that used tax revenue to raise benefits for individuals who had a low pension because they earned a low income. Although an attempt to elucidate a minimum benefit is welcome, the debate has yet to get off the ground because the DPJ has sidestepped the key issue, the level of the overall benefit.

In Korea, in conjunction with expanding the coverage rate, premiums are being raised and the replacement rate is being lowered to make the public pension system more sustainable. The premium began at 3 percent of a worker's income when the system was launched in 1988, but it was raised to 6 percent in 1993 and then to 9 percent in 1998.[10] The replacement rate was initially 70 percent, but it was lowered to 60 percent in 1999 and to 50 percent in 2007. It is scheduled to be lowered by 0.5 percentage point annually from 2008 until 2027 and to stabilize at 40 percent from 2028 on.[11] Simultaneously, in 2007 Korea introduced a basic old-age pension system, a means-tested guaranteed minimum pension funded by general tax revenues.

In Korea, participants must be enrolled for twenty years to receive basic pension benefits and for forty years to receive full pension benefits. Because the system was launched in 1988, the benefit reductions took place before the full-fledged benefit payments began. Actions were taken early and that probably helped to push through such relatively steep reductions in the replacement rate.

---

8. Japan Ministry of Health, Labor, and Welfare (2005). Dollar equivalents are based on the exchange rate on January 24, 2011.

9. A model household is defined as including a couple, one of whom is a single earner enrolled for forty years, and two children. The definition has been criticized as no longer describing the standard household.

10. National Pension Service website (www.nps.or.kr/jsppage/english/scheme/scheme_02.jsp).

11. Park (2009).

Coverage of Public Pensions

The Chinese government has not always clearly elucidated the replacement rate of its basic endowment insurance, but the Organization for Economic Cooperation and Development estimates the rate to be 35 percent for the common pool and 24.2 percent for private accounts, for a total of 59.2 percent.[12] On the surface, it appears that China's public pension is maintaining a replacement rate on par with the OECD average. The problem, however, lies in China's low pension coverage rate—that is, the low percentage of Chinese people who are enrolled in the pension program. That makes comparison with other countries less meaningful.

No matter how attractive the terms of the pension are, limited participation makes it difficult to give China's pension system a high score for adequacy. The coverage rate is an especially important metric for public pensions. Both Japan and Korea have incrementally raised the coverage rate of their public pensions, and although it is not perfect, they maintain a certain level of coverage. Japan began with occupational pensions and expanded coverage by introducing a national pension for the self-employed and others. Japan's introduction of a basic pension in 1985 served to create a link among the national pension, EPI, and mutual aid pensions, which until then had been independently operated. The 1985 reforms also expanded coverage to dependent spouses, whose participation had been voluntary until then. Korea, too, has incrementally expanded the coverage of its public pension. When it was launched in 1988, the pension covered employees of business establishments with at least ten full-time employees, but it gradually included smaller firms, and by 2006 coverage was extended to all workplaces with at least one employee. The self-employed, farmers, fishermen, and irregular employees also are covered.

China's basic endowment insurance covers only 20.5 percent of the labor force, well below the OECD average of 83.3 percent, and raising the public pension coverage rate is likely to become the next urgent issue for China.[13] Whether the current replacement rate is sustainable with higher coverage will then be the issue.

Examining the Presence of Private Pensions in Terms of Assets

Only private pensions can fill the void that will be created by reducing the role of public pensions. In fact, the strengthening of private pensions is a trend that can be seen in a number of countries, including Germany, which introduced its

---

12. Nomura Institute of Capital Markets Research (2007).
13. Nomura Institute of Capital Markets Research (2007).

Figure 2-2. *Comparison of Private Pensions as a Percent of GDP with Public Pension Replacement Rates*[a]

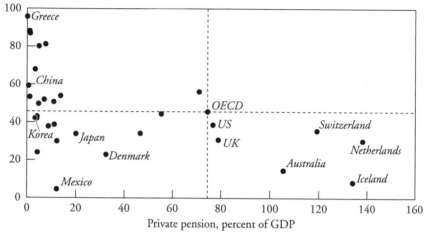

Public pension gross replacement rate

Private pension, percent of GDP

Source: Nomura Institute of Capital Markets Research, based on OECD data.

a. The gross replacement rate is the gross pension entitlement divided by gross pre-retirement earnings. Public pensions are pensions operated by the government and do not include mandatory private pensions. Private pensions relative to GDP are based on 2007 numbers.

Riester pension at the same time that it lowered the replacement rate of its public pension, and the United Kingdom, which positioned its public pension as a guaranteed minimum and introduced a stakeholder pension that is easily accessible by low-income individuals who are not enrolled in a corporate pension.

As shown in table 2-2, the public pension replacement rate in both Japan and Korea will drop considerably. To examine the presence of private pensions in Japan and Korea, we look at the amount of private pension assets as a percentage of GDP.

Figure 2-2 plots private pension assets as a percentage of GDP on the horizontal axis and the gross replacement rate for public pensions on the vertical axis. The OECD averages are a replacement rate of 45.7 percent and private pension assets totaling 74.5 percent of GDP. That replacement rate is lower than the 59 percent noted above because the 59 percent includes benefits from private pensions with mandatory enrollment (like Australia's Superannuation) as well as private pensions that are not mandatory but that have nearly full participation (such as the occupational pension in the Netherlands). Figure 2-2, on the other hand, shows the replacement rate for public pensions narrowly defined.

The lower-right quadrant of the graph indicates a limited role for public pensions and a large presence for private pensions, whereas the upper-left quadrant presents the opposite pattern, a large role for public pensions and a small presence for private pensions. What is important is to have some system in place for old age, whether it is a public pension, a private pension, or a combination of the two. Ultimately each country has a choice of whether to emphasize the public or the private option.

The lower-left quadrant indicates both a weak role for public pensions and a small presence for private pensions and therefore an overall inferior level of pension adequacy. It comes down to deciding whether to shift to the right (in the graph) by expanding private pensions or to shift upward by expanding public pensions. The direction of the reforms taken in many Western countries has been rightward—that is, toward expansion of private pensions.

Both Japan and Korea lie in the lower-left quadrant. As to whether there has been a visible shift from public pensions to private pensions in Korea, its recent introduction of a corporate pension system should be viewed positively as a first step in that direction. The same probably could be said for China. On the other hand, viewed from the perspective of private pension assets relative to GDP, private pensions do not have a very large presence in Japan, despite its nearly fifty-year history of corporate pensions, dating back to the introduction of tax-qualified pension plans in 1961. Policy measures to strengthen the role of private pensions seem to be limited. A reform accompanying the public pension reforms of 2004 slightly increased the maximum contribution to DC plans based on the scheduled future declines in the replacement rate of the EPI, but given that the maximum contribution of DC plans was fairly low to begin with and was not raised by very much, that policy change was not seen as a measure that would substantially increase the level of private pension assets.[14]

Corporate pension assets totaled approximately ¥61 trillion ($738 billion) as of March 2009, or 12 percent of GDP, in Japan; 10.3 trillion won ($9 billion) as of November 2009, or 7.9 percent of GDP, in Korea; and 191.1 billion yuan ($29 billion) as of 2008, or less than 1 percent of GDP, in China.[15]

Coverage of Corporate Pension Plans

An important measure besides the level of private pension assets is the coverage of corporate pensions. Before looking at that, it is important to see whether

---

14. Nomura (2009a).

15. Data from Japan Pension Fund Association, Korea Financial Supervisory Service, and Sekine and Nomura (2009).

corporate pensions are mandatory or voluntary. Countries that have introduced private pensions with mandatory enrollment include Australia, Denmark, Sweden, and Switzerland.

Prior to introducing corporate pensions, Korea required companies with at least five employees to offer a lump-sum retirement pay system. When retirement pensions were introduced in December 2005, that requirement was changed to offering a lump-sum retirement pay system, a retirement pension plan, or both.

According to a January 2010 report from Korea's Ministry of Employment and Labor, 1.723 million workers (22.6 percent of all employees at workplaces with at least five employees) had enrolled in a retirement pension plan from the time that the plans were launched to November 2009. The plans are now offered by 67,705 companies, 13 percent of the companies eligible.[16] The company participation rate and the employee enrollment rates indicate that larger companies are ahead in offering retirement pensions. It seems that Korea has been fairly successful in spreading pension plans, achieving an enrollment rate of more than 20 percent after only four years.

Korea also plans on eliminating the exception for companies with fewer than five employees effective January 2011, at which point all business establishments would be obligated to offer either a lump-sum retirement pay system or a retirement pension plan. At the same time, to encourage people to choose the corporate pension over the lump-sum payout, the Korea Workers' Compensation and Welfare Service (COMWEL) is scheduled to offer low-income workers a pension plan with low fees.[17]

Corporate pensions are voluntary in Japan and China, where each company makes its own decision on whether to offer one. For Japan, it is necessary to understand the corporate pension reforms of 2001 to gauge the current status of corporate pension provision. There used to be only two types of corporate pension schemes in Japan, the tax-qualified pension plans, introduced in 1961, and the Employees' Pension Fund, introduced in 1965. TQPPs were introduced to promote the accumulation of funds outside the company, because the lump-sum retirement payouts that had been common at the time were being funded by book reserves. The EPF substitutes for a portion of the EPI, the public pension program for private sector employees. Typically, part of the EPI premium is paid into the

16. Korea Ministry of Employment and Labor, "Pension Fund Reserve Reaches 10 Trillion Won," January 14, 2010 (www.moel.go.kr/english/topic/working_view.jsp?&idx=484).
17. COMWEL is a government agency that offers welfare services to small businesses. Revisions to Korea's pension scheme are discussed in Korea International Labor Foundation, "Retirement Benefit System to Cover All the Workplaces from December 1, 2010," *Labor Today,* September 16, 2010.

EPF, the employer makes an additional contribution, and the fund is managed toward the benefit payment.

Japan's corporate pension reforms of 2001 included a ten-year phaseout of TQPPs by March 2012, because the plans were deemed to have insufficient funding standards to ensure pension benefits. DB corporate pension plans and DC pensions were introduced in 2001. The expectation at the time was that during the ten years before TQPPs were eliminated, they would be rolled over to DBCP plans, to DC plans, or to small and medium enterprise retirement allowance cooperatives.[18] What appears to have happened, however, is that roughly half of the companies canceled their TQPPs without rolling them over into another retirement plan. With no data available to adjust for people covered by multiple plans, the figures presented here are simple totals of the number of participants in each plan. That number declined from over 20 million in FY2001 to about 17 million today.[19] That is equivalent to roughly 50 percent of all salaried employees in the private sector, and after participation in multiple plans is taken into account, it is likely that less than half of the Japanese workforce actually participates in a pension plan. Although that is seen as a problem, an effective solution has yet to be proposed.

When China instituted public pension reforms in the 1990s, it promoted corporate pensions as a way to provide a multi-pillar pension system. After issuing numerous circulars related to corporate pensions, the government established a new system of corporate pensions with the enactment in 2004 of two regulations on occupational pensions. Companies that want to offer the new corporate pensions first have to prove their participation in the already obligatory basic endowment insurance and then go through an approval process that includes a thorough inspection by the Ministry of Labor and Social Security. The first companies approved to offer the new corporate pensions were the Bank of China, China Everbright Bank, and PICC Property and Casualty Company. Until the end of 2008, 33,000 companies introduced corporate pensions covering a total of 10.38 million employees.[20] There has already been strong growth in the number of participants, and further growth is expected in light of the large number of those eligible.

Both Japan and Korea have already made clear their intention to lower the replacement rate of their public pensions, a change that will lead to public pensions having a smaller role, but it is not yet clear whether private pensions will grow

18. These cooperatives constituted a public plan for smaller firms that would have difficulty offering a retirement payout scheme on their own.

19. Calculated with data from the Japan Pension Fund Association and the Ministry of Health, Labor, and Welfare.

20. Sekine and Nomura (2009).

enough to make up the difference. That being said, Korea moved quickly to lower its replacement rate while at the same time introducing a minimum benefit. In so doing, it has signaled a clearer change of course based on shifting public pensions into the role of providing minimum guarantees while giving private pensions the role of replacing income earned during the working years. As noted, over 20 percent of eligible Korean employees had enrolled in corporate pensions only four years after their introduction. The growth in corporate pension assets is another thing to observe, which some forecast to reach 30 trillion won ($25 billion) by the end of 2010.[21]

While many observers question the assumptions underlying the forecast that Japan's replacement rate of 50 percent will be maintained in the future, that issue remains ambiguous because no official discussions have been initiated. The role of the basic pension also remains ambiguous. There is a possibility that such ambiguities have the effect of keeping both companies and individuals from fully sensing the urgency of making their own provisions for retirement.

The Gap with Western Economies

Once private pensions become more important and are recognized as a main supplement to public pensions, the nexus of serious debate should shift to coverage rates, even if participation in private pensions is voluntary. In the countries with voluntary participation—Canada, the United States, the United Kingdom, Ireland, and Germany—the coverage rate of private pension plans including corporate pensions is over 50 percent, but even that is considered insufficient (figure 2-3).

One approach to increase coverage rates of voluntary private pensions recently tried in some countries is known as "soft compulsion," which consists of automatic enrollment in a defined contribution plan from which the employee can opt out. Pension reforms in the United Kingdom in 2007 and 2008 required all employers to automatically enroll employees in a pension plan while offering them the option of not participating. Those reforms also provided for establishing the National Employment Savings Trust (NEST) as a repository of retirement savings for employees without a pension plan at their workplace, and preparations are being made to launch NEST in 2012. In the United States, the Obama administration has proposed introducing automatic IRA enrollment.[22]

Automatic enrollment answers the question of what the initial default setting of a retirement plan should be. By changing the default setting from nonparticipation to participation, plans can increase the participation rate substantially, as is now

---

21. Kim Da-ye, "Your After-Retirement Nest Egg at Stake," *Korea Times*, August 16, 2010.
22. Nomura (2009b).

Figure 2-3. *Coverage Rates of Voluntary Private Pensions*

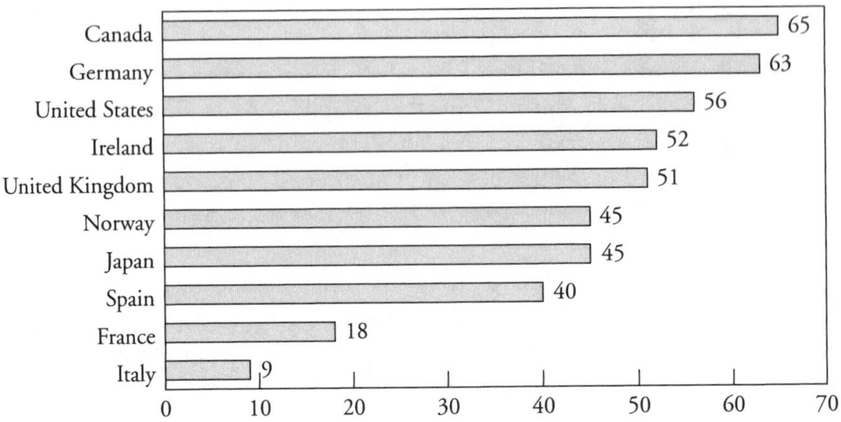

Source: OECD (2007).

being witnessed in U.S. 401(k) plans. Although the concept of automatic enrollment has yet to arrive in Japan, using an automatic enrollment mechanism on
individual DC plans as envisioned in the United Kingdom could give a major
boost to the percentage of employees covered by private pensions in Japan as well.

In fact, a reform bill submitted in 2010 to the Diet in Korea proposes requiring newly established companies to offer their employees a corporate pension
instead of a lump-sum retirement pay system unless specifically requested by the
employees to do otherwise.[23] Under the current Employee Retirement Benefit
Security Act, those employers who have not established a retirement pension plan
are deemed to have chosen to introduce a lump-sum retirement payout program.
In other words, the current default setting is the lump-sum retirement pay system.
The proposal could be seen as an attempt to change the default setting to corporate pension enrollment for companies establishing new plans.

Increasing Levels of Prefunding

The next issue is how the trend toward increasing prefunding is materializing
in each of the three countries. Prefunding can take various forms. China has introduced a funded defined contribution scheme as part of its public pension system.

23. Korea Ministry of Employment and Labor, "Pension Fund Reserve Reaches 10 Trillion Won,"
January 14, 2010.

It has also established a reserve fund as a buffer for the future benefit payment. Japanese and Korean public pension systems are pay-as-you-go, but they have large reserve funds. All three countries invest their reserve funds in the market.

China's Partially Funded Public Pension System

China has been the most explicit with its introduction of a partially funded public pension system. Employees in China contribute 8 percent of their wages to an individual account within the basic endowment insurance. The employer's contribution, 20 percent of wages, goes into the common fund, and upon retirement employees receive benefits from both the common fund and their individual account.

This system is similar to the one in Sweden, where 16 percent of the 18.5 percent premium goes into a PAYGO notional DC plan and the remaining 2.5 percent goes into a funded individual account. The main difference is that in China the assets in the individual accounts are not managed by each employee. The individual accounts earn interest based on the rate paid on bank deposits, and assets are invested in both bank deposits and government bonds. In 2006, nine provinces entrusted management of the investment accounts to the National Social Security Fund.

The use of individual accounts within basic endowment insurance puts China's among the frontrunners of the world's public pension schemes, although it must deal with the problem of "empty accounts." That term refers to the diversion of funds from individual accounts to the common fund, which suffers from chronic deficits owing to the aging of the population and insufficient contributions. One cannot say that China has established a truly funded system of individual accounts until there is a clear separation between the common fund and the individual accounts, with the funds designated for the individual accounts accumulating separately.

Large Public Pension Reserve Funds

One characteristic that the public pension funds of Japan, Korea, and China have in common is that all have reserve funds that are invested in the market. Japan's Government Pension Investment Fund is the world's largest pension fund, with assets totaling $1.3 trillion in 2009, more than triple the size of the next-largest fund, Norway's Government Pension Fund–Global. Korea's National Pension Fund had assets in 2009 totaling $235 billion, behind the reserve funds of Norway and the Netherlands. According to Korea's NPF, its assets are now building up and are expected to total $2 trillion by 2043. China's National Social Security Fund was established in 2000 to facilitate the future financing of basic endowment insurance. Its assets are growing rapidly as well; after less than ten years in existence, it was already in the global top twenty of pension funds, with assets of $114 billion in 2009 (table 2-3).

A number of developed countries have pursued a policy of establishing reserve funds for public pensions. In 2001, for example, France established its FRR (Fonds de Réserve pour les Retraites) and Ireland its NPRF (National Pension Reserve Fund) with the aim of slicing off a portion of the national wealth to address the future pressures on pension benefits that will arise from the mass retirement of baby boomers. Norway's Government Pension Fund–Global, which was restructured in 1996, has a similar objective. Payment into these reserve funds comes from such sources as proceeds from the sale of oil or privatization of government-owned entities or from general revenues (budget surplus), and no payments from the funds are expected until around 2020. The funds are independent from pension finance for the time being and are being positioned purely as surplus funds.

In the late 1990s, both Canada and Sweden greatly revamped their existing reserve funds, positioning them as critical to maintaining the sustainability of public pensions. Reserve funds in Canada and Sweden are composed of surplus collected pension premiums. Pension financing (liability side) virtually determines the required rate of return. Pure surplus funds like FRR, NPRF, and Norway's Government Pension Fund and funds from surplus premiums are essentially the same in that they are eventually paid out as pension benefits, although the pure surplus funds tend to have a greater degree of investment freedom.

Among Japan, Korea, and China, China established a pure surplus fund, the National Social Security Fund, in 2000 in preparation for future increases in pension benefits, as did France and Ireland. The NSSF's funding comes from central government revenues, revenues from the sale of state-owned enterprise stocks, and profits from the lottery. On the other hand, Japan's GPIF invests surplus pension premiums. Korea's NPF also invests surplus pension premiums, but because the public pension is still immature, it is very close to being a pure surplus fund for the time being.

Based on the above discussion, all three countries are either current with or even a step ahead of the global trend in terms of building public pension reserve funds. But it is necessary to look closely at how each manages its pension reserve assets, because that has a major impact on the sustainability of a public pension scheme.

Investment Guidelines and Actual Investment of Public Pension Assets

When public pension reserve funds are invested in the market, it normally is considered appropriate to pursue a prudent return on risk based on the standards

Table 2-3. *World's Largest Pension Funds*[a]

2009 rank	2008 rank	Fund	Country	Fund type	Total assets (US$ millions)
1	1	Government Pension Investment	Japan	National	1,315,071
2	2	Government Pension Fund-Global	Norway	National	475,859
3	3	ABP	Netherlands	Government employees	299,873
4	6	National Pension	Korea	National	234,946
5	5	Federal Retirement Thrift[b]	U.S.	Government employees	234,404
6	4	California Public Employees[b]	U.S.	Government employees	198,765
7	7	Local Government Officials[c]	Japan	Government employees	164,510
8	9	California State Teachers[b]	U.S.	Government employees	130,461
9	10	New York State Common[b]	U.S.	Government employees	125,692
10	17	PFZW	Netherlands	Private	123,390
11	16	Central Provident Fund[d]	Singapore	National	122,497
12	23	Canada Pension[d]	Canada	National	122,067
13	12	Florida State Board	U.S.	Government employees	114,663
14	24	National Social Security	China	National	113,716
15	11	Pension Fund Association[c]	Japan	Private	113,364
16	14	ATP	Denmark	National	111,887
17	15	New York City Retirement[b]	U.S.	Government employees	111,669
18	29	GEPF[d]	South Africa	Government employees	110,976
19	18	Employees Provident Fund	Malaysia	National	109,002
20	13	General Motors	U.S.	Private	99,200

Source: Nomura Institute of Capital Markets Research, based on data from Pensions and Investments (www.pionline.com/article/20100906/CHART1/100839991/-1/WWTOPFUNDS).

a. U.S. Social Security is not included because it does not invest in the market.
b. September 2009.
c. Estimate.
d. March 2010.

of conduct for institutional investors. Such standards are especially important for public pension reserve funds because of the general perception that investment of such assets may be susceptible to political intervention. In other words, there is a risk that the funds will be diverted from their true objective—financing pension benefits—and used to finance investments in economic development, thereby lowering the returns that they might otherwise generate. In addition to reserve funds being diverted directly to public investments, they can be used to purchase government securities yielding below-market rates, which is not in keeping with the standards of behavior for institutional investors either. Other examples of political interference include use of pension assets to defend against the acquisition of critical domestic industries by foreign interests and, conversely, the prohibition against investing in companies based in countries that have sour diplomatic relations with the investing government.

Because of the perceived vulnerability of reserve assets to political interference, it is important that pension assets be managed according to investment guidelines based on legislated investment objectives and established by the national pension authorities. In addition, as described later, a governance structure should be put in place to keep government intervention in check.

Before discussing the governance issues, let us look at the investment policies for pension reserve funds in Japan, Korea, and China. Those for Japan's GPIF call for safe and efficient investments with a long-term horizon and try to ensure the investment yield required to finance expected benefit payouts. That may be somewhat conservative, but it is a fairly typical way of phrasing the investment policy. China's policies are similar, calling for specialized and standardized investments that are safe and responsible. The investment principles spelled out by Korea's NPF, on the other hand, could be construed as having wider objectives, namely,

—Stability: The fund should pursue a sustainable level of profit to achieve stability of the fund and the national economy as well.

—Profitability: The fund should play a role in the social safety net and contribute to the growth of the national economy as a supplier of long-term capital. The fund is to be managed based on the principle of maximizing returns within the constraint of not harming its stability.

—Public benefit and welfare: In addition to maintaining both stability and profitability, the fund should have a positive impact on the national economy and contribute to the public benefit and welfare, such as by providing social infrastructure.

—Liquidity: Measures that ensure liquidity in order to achieve stable benefit payments should be considered in the future.

—Independence: Abiding by the investment principles is the best way to fulfill the long-term interests of all stakeholders.

Including achieving a stable national economy, contributing to growth in the national economy, and having a positive impact on the national economy while contributing to the public benefit and welfare among these objectives indicates that investment decisions may be based on considerations besides risk-return parameters.[24]

However, when Korea's two major life insurance companies, Korean Life and Samsung Life, had IPOs in March 2010, the NPF did not subscribe because it deemed the IPO price too high. Immediately prior to Korean Life's IPO, the NPF had revised its internal rules regarding equity investments to allow investing in IPOs, a move that was seen as paving the way for its participation in large-scale IPOs. That made its decision not to subscribe all the more surprising. National Pension Service chairman Jun Kwang-woo made the following comments in an interview: "I think the Korea Life case shows our principles. The pricing was too high, and we had no other reason to consider the deal under such terms, so we didn't buy. We will take the same professional approach in judging the IPO of Samsung Life."[25]

One more observation that can be made about Korea's NPF is that under Chairman Jun, who was appointed to his post in 2009, it has aggressively invested in alternative vehicles. Figure 2-4 shows the asset allocations of the three countries' public pension reserve funds. Like Japan, Korea has a high allocation to domestic bonds, but unlike Japan, it allocates 4 percent to alternative investments. By 2014 the NPF plans to lower its allocation for domestic bonds in its medium-term asset allocation plan to 60 percent from 78 percent and instead to raise its allocations for foreign bonds from 4 to 10 percent, for domestic equity from 12 to 20 percent, for foreign equity from 2 to 10 percent, and for alternative investments from 4 to 10 percent.[26] While each country has its own definition of alternative investments, if Korea follows its medium-term plan, its allocation to alternative investments will be at a level not far from that of the public pension reserve management organizations such as Sweden's AP Funds, the Canada Pension Plan Investment Board (CPPIB), and Ireland's NPRF.

24. NPS investment policy is disclosed on its website: see National Pension Fund, "Investment Policies" (www.nps.or.kr/jsppage/english/npf_korea/npf_01_02.jsp).

25. Cho Jin-seo, "Pension Fund to Boost Overseas Investment," *Korea Times,* March 11, 2010.

26. Compared with asset allocation as of 2008. Korea National Pension Service, "Korea National Pension Fund," June 2009 (www.nps.or.kr/jsppage/english/npf_korea/npf_06_01.jsp).

Figure 2-4. *Management of Pension Assets by the GPIF, NPF, and NSSF*
Percent

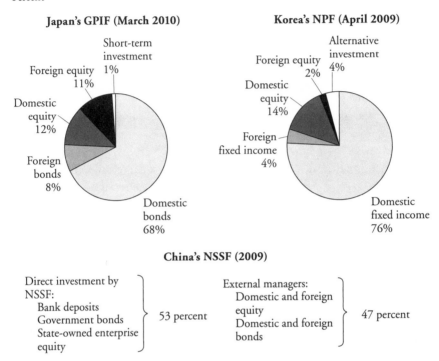

Japan's GPIF (March 2010)

Foreign equity
11%

Domestic
equity
12%

Foreign
bonds
8%

Short-term
investment
1%

Domestic
bonds
68%

Korea's NPF (April 2009)

Foreign equity
2%

Alternative
investment
4%

Domestic
equity
14%

Foreign
fixed income
4%

Domestic
fixed income
76%

China's NSSF (2009)

Direct investment by
NSSF:
    Bank deposits
    Government bonds   } 53 percent
    State-owned enterprise
    equity

External managers:
    Domestic and foreign
    equity   } 47 percent
    Domestic and foreign
    bonds

Source: Nomura Institute of Capital Markets Research, based on disclosures from Japan's Government Pension Investment Fund (GPIF), Korea's National Pension Fund (NPF), and China's National Social Security Fund (NSSF).

Governance Structures of Public Pension Reserve Management Organizations

As noted, the management of public pension reserve assets can be vulnerable to political influence, and to ensure freedom from such pressure it is considered desirable to have a governance structure that separates the governing body from the group that carries out day-to-day investment management. The governing body would be charged with approving investment policies and other key issues, and the asset management group would report its activities to the governing body rather than to the government. The governing body would thus serve as a buffer between the government and the asset management group. Given the debates on pension governance such as at the World Bank and OECD, that appears to be the

Figure 2-5. *Public Pension Reserve Fund Management Organization,*
with a Governing Body

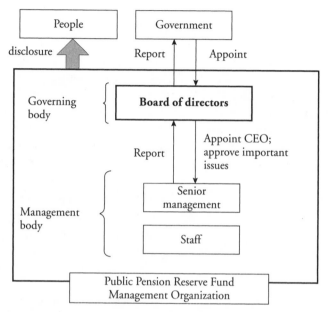

Source: Nomura Institute of Capital Markets Research.

approach to governance of public pension asset management currently accepted
by many developed countries (figure 2-5).[27]

The more diverse the pension investments, the more important the governance
structure. Take, for example, a portfolio that focuses on just domestic bonds
and/or passive stock investments, and one that also invests overseas and includes
alternative investments. The degree of conflict of interest and the complexity of
decisions will no doubt be greater for the latter.

The organizations managing the national pensions in Japan, Korea, and China
all appear to have some shortcomings in terms of their independence from the
government. Korea's NPF and China's NSSF have boards of directors as their
main governing entity, as do comparable funds in developed countries. The governing bodies of organizations managing reserve funds can be broadly classified
into two types: "stakeholder participation bodies," in which labor, management,

27. Nomura (2008).

and other stakeholders have representation, and "specialist bodies," which comprise financial and pension specialists. Korea's NPF management committee is basically composed of stakeholder participants, with its twenty members including three employer representatives, three employee representatives, six representatives of the self-employed, and two specialists. Apparently, its structure is quite similar to France's FRR. The chairman of the NPF management committee, however, is the minister of health, welfare, and family affairs, the head of the government ministry that supervises the National Pension Service. Having the head of the supervisory agency also serve as the head of the governing body of the organization managing the reserve fund limits the degree of autonomy from the government.

The board of China's NSSF also has twenty members, including active high-ranking government officials (vice ministers). The top four members of the asset management body (chairman and vice chairmen) also are members. The deputy head of a labor union and an academic (head of the Development Research Center of the State Council) are members as well, but the presence of government officials on the board limits its autonomy from the government. Also, there is a lack of clarity over the division of roles and relationship with the asset management body, as the top four members of the asset management body are also members of the board.

Of the three countries, however, Japan deviates most from what could be considered the global standard for governance structure of pension fund reserves. Japan's GPIF does not have the equivalent of a governing body. The chairman of the GPIF is the head of the asset management body and holds the bulk of the decisionmaking authority related to GPIF operations. Although there is an investment committee composed of specialists, it serves in a purely advisory capacity, with neither the rights nor the responsibilities of management.

Problems with the GPIF's governance structure already have been recognized in Japan. A committee established in November 2009 to study how the GPIF is run has been looking at how basic investment policy is decided; how assets are invested (asset classes; active versus passive investments); what structure for the governance of investments is used; whether the fund, which is frequently criticized as having become too large, should be divided; and whether socially responsible investment principles should be followed. However, the committee's final report issued in December 2010 did not go beyond presenting both sides of the argument on most of those issues, although it presented some consensus views on how to revise the governance structure of the GPIF.[28]

---

28. Japan Ministry of Health, Labor, and Welfare (2010).

The impact that governance structure has on investment performance was pointed out in Ambachtsheer (2007). In light of the current view that a board is the best form of governing body, it is clear that all three countries have some changes to make to improve the governance structure of their public pension reserve funds.

Japan's Public Pension Reform and Reserve Fund

Although the governance structure of its GPIF is not ideal, Japan is actually ahead of many countries in that it has built up a large public pension reserve fund and it has been investing in the market. However, it was decided in the public pension reform of 2004 to reduce pension reserves over the next 100 years from the equivalent of five years of pension benefit costs at the time of the reform to just one year of benefit costs.[29] As noted earlier, the 2004 reforms fixed the maximum pension premium while lowering the replacement rate through a demographics-based adjustment of the benefits. By drawing down reserves, premium increases and benefit reductions will be moderated. The basic thinking behind the reform was that the role of pension reserves was to contribute to the stabilization of pension financing while controlling premium increases and keeping benefits as high as possible.

There is no consensus, including at the global level, of what constitutes the right level of public pension reserves.[30] It is difficult to say at this point whether Japan's decision to lower its level of reserves (vis-à-vis the benefit payment amount) should be viewed as contrary to the current trend or whether the level of Japan's reserve fund is ahead of the times and therefore can now be reduced to lower levels over the long term.

The Shift to DC Plans and Improvement of Sustainability

Historically the pension systems of many countries have been defined benefit plans, but there has been a shift in recent years to defined contribution plans. One reason is that many companies have learned the difficulty of providing a DB plan, as much as they might like to do so. The existence of DC plans as an alternative makes it possible for companies not to give up completely on the idea of providing a corporate pension. Achieving a smooth transition from DB plans to DC plans is another critical element in making private pensions more sustainable as a whole.

29. Japan Ministry of Health, Labor, and Welfare (2005).
30. Ono (2007).

Both DB plans and DC plans have advantages and drawbacks. However, by skillfully combining the two schemes in a way that meets their own needs, companies are able to diversify their pension schemes. From the perspective of a country as a whole, that will result in a greater number of companies providing private pensions in a more balanced manner.

Among corporations in Western countries, those in the United States have shown the most pronounced shift from DB to DC plans. DB plans used to be the primary form of corporate pension, but the number of such plans as well as the number of participants peaked in the mid-1980s and has been declining ever since. Measured in assets under management, DB plans were overtaken in the latter half of the 1990s by DC plans. Today 401(k) plans have become the most popular form of corporate pensions in the United States.[31] This change has been fueled not only by changes in the economy and society, including changes in industrial structure and an increasingly mobile labor market, but also by measures introduced to strengthen defined benefit plans, including stricter funding standards, the introduction of pension benefit insurance, and stronger disclosure requirements based on pension accounting standards. Since around 2005, even large companies that had provided both DB and DC plans have been freezing the former,[32] perhaps motivated by a number of factors, such as an increasingly volatile investment environment; radical changes in the global competitive landscape, including the severe pressure from emerging markets; and the shift to immediate recognition of pension funding in pension accounting.

There also has been a shift to DC plans in European countries, like the United Kingdom, that have well-developed occupational pensions, for reasons similar to those in the United States. Other countries, such as France, Italy, and Spain, that traditionally have relied heavily on public pensions are turning to DC plans for newly introduced pension plans to offset what is seen as the unavoidable shrinkage of public pensions. Numerous other countries, including Denmark, Sweden, and some countries in central Europe, are starting to use DC plans for private pensions with mandatory enrollment. All those changes combined are leading to growth in the size of DC pension plans. A survey by the European Federation for Retirement Provision (EFRP) in March 2010 found that DC plans had 58 million participants and assets of €1.3 trillion ($1.8 trillion). With both France and Italy planning to introduce measures to expand eligibility and raise contribution rates, the growth trend in DC plans is expected to continue.[33]

31. Based on the analysis of data published in U.S. Department of Labor, "Private Pension Plan Bulletin."
32. Nomura (2006).
33. EFRP (2010).

Table 2-4. *Assets under Management in Defined Benefit and Defined Contribution Plans in Japan and Korea*

Country	DB plans	DC plans	Individual DC plans
Japan			
Number of firms	—	13,222	—
Number of participants	13,620,000	3,572,000	114,136
Total assets (¥ trillions)	57	3.7	0.3
(US$ billions)	689.9	44.8	3.6
Korea			
Number of firms	18,926	27,067	21,712
Number of participants	1,172,344	472,854	77,464
Total assets (won trillions)	6.8	2.6	0.9
(US$ billions)	6.1	2.3	0.8

Source: Nomura Institute of Capital Markets Research, based on Korea Ministry of Employment and Labor; Japan Ministry of Labor, Health, and Welfare; and the Japan Association of DC Plan Administrators.

The Situation in Japan, Korea, and China

As was the case with public pensions, China is adopting more aggressive policies than Japan and Korea, namely by introducing the funded DC format in its public pensions. In addition, the only new corporate pensions that China allows are DC plans, a policy choice aimed at avoiding the limitations of DB plans and the cost of switching from DB plans to DC plans experienced in the United States and Europe.

Both Japan and Korea have only defined benefit public pensions, but they offer private pensions in both DB and DC versions. When it introduced corporate pensions in 2005, Korea made both DB and DC plans available. It also implemented special measures for small businesses and introduced individual retirement accounts as a way to ensure the portability of pensions.[34] As of November 2009, DB plans had a greater share of both participants and assets under management, as shown in table 2-4. Some observers attribute that to the introduction of DB pension plans by large corporations.

Japan introduced DC pension plans for the first time in 2001. There are two types, corporate plans established by companies for their employees to join, and individual plans in which the self-employed and others can enroll. The reasons for the introduction of DC plans can be traced back to the 1990s, when a weak

34. Korea treats companies with nine or fewer employees, all of whom have opened an IRA, as having offered a corporate pension.

Japanese stock market and weak economy made it more difficult for corporations to contribute to their pension plans, while at the same time the introduction of new pension accounting rules made the funding status of defined benefit plans more transparent. After DC plans were introduced in 2001, they gradually caught on, both with large corporations and with smaller firms. DC plans had 3.572 million participants by May 2010 and were offered by 13,222 companies as of June 2010. The number of participants has increased steadily, but it is still small compared with the number in DB plans, which have a simple total of roughly 14 million participants (not adjusted for participation in multiple plans). The gap in assets under management is even greater, at ¥57 trillion ($690 billion) in DB plans and only ¥3.7 trillion ($48 billion) in DC plans as of March 2009 (table 2-4).

With public pensions expected to shrink, strengthening of DC plans is probably the only way to boost the growth of private pensions. However, there are numerous problems with Japan's current rules on DC pensions, including the low contribution amounts allowed, the limited scope of people eligible to enroll, and the very strict rules governing early withdrawals. Reforms are needed to address those problems so that Japan's DC plans can grow to their potential.

One development common to both Japan and Korea that could cause a shift to DC plans in the near future is convergence with or adoption of the International Financial Reporting Standards (IFRS). Korea will start requiring the application of IFRS in 2011. Japan plans to make a decision by 2012 on whether it will adopt IFRS, but whatever the decision, the convergence of Japan's accounting standards with IFRS will continue. A shift is under way toward immediate recognition of pension funding on financial statements, without any multi-year smoothing adjustments. What that means is that the impact from fluctuations in interest rates and stock prices on pension funding must be reflected each year on the balance sheet.

Looking back, Japan's introduction of pension accounting in FY2000 spurred large companies to begin offering DC plans. The shift that is now under way toward immediate recognition of pension funding status is expected to motivate Japanese companies to revise their own pension plans yet again. In Korea, too, attention is focused on how the requirement to apply IFRS may affect employers' choice of pension plans.

Corporate Pension Contributions and Investment

If the shift from DB plans to DC plans is going to ultimately contribute to the sustainability of corporate pensions, it is imperative that DC plans ensure that appropriate contributions are made and that the assets are invested properly. Although it is difficult to stipulate what contributions and investments are "appropriate," it is generally accepted that ensuring reasonable contributions and investments over a long period is more difficult for DC plans, given the large role that participants, who are not pension investment professionals, have in making decisions on contributions and investments. As the shift into DC plans gains momentum in the United States and Europe, debate over how to deal with the irrationality of participant behavior is heating up.

Until the 1990s, the most common approach to 401(k) plans in the United States was to rely on employees who joined the plans based on their understanding of the advantages to make their own investment decisions for their own personal accounts, after receiving some basic investment education. As it turned out, however, on average about 30 percent of employees did not enroll even after the advantages were explained to them, and it also became clear that it was unrealistic to assume that all participants would act as rational investors. The Pension Protection Act of 2006 legislated some automatic mechanisms, namely automatic enrollment and automatic increases in the contribution rate. In addition, the act (and regulation thereafter) made clear that as long as the selection process for the default product was appropriate, the employer would not be responsible for investment losses, even when a product with the potential for a loss in principal was chosen as the default product. The general view is that more employees will be automatically enrolled in 401(k) plans and their investments will be in the default product. Currently target-date funds are the most popular default product for plans with automatic enrollment.[35]

A variety of approaches to contributions and investments are seen in DC plans in Europe. In some cases, employers are obligated to match contributions made by participants, and in other cases the contribution level is set by group-level negotiation, with labor and management each contributing. On the investment side, according the EFRP survey mentioned above, 60 percent of plans offer participants a choice of at least two investments, while 40 percent of plans do not offer participants a choice; in the United Kingdom, Denmark, and Sweden, 80 to 90 percent of participants who were given a choice wound up investing in the default products, half of which were life-cycle funds.[36]

Japan, Korea, and China still have a gap with Europe and the United States in several respects with regard to the trends in corporate pension contributions and investments. In Korea, corporations are required by the Employee Retirement Benefit Security Act to make contributions, and participants are allowed to make additional contributions. Because neither firms nor their employees are yet comfortable with pension investing, at this point there are restrictions on how pension

35. Nomura (2006).
36. EFRP (2010).

assets can be allocated. Even for DB plans, maximum allocations are 30 percent for listed domestic and overseas stocks, 50 percent for equity funds, 50 percent for balanced funds, and 50 percent for overseas bond funds. DC plans for which the employee directs the investment have even stricter rules, with no investment allowed in individual stocks, equity funds, or balanced funds. The only allowed investments are deposit accounts, insurance products (with guaranteed principal), and funds with no higher than a 40 percent equity allocation.[37] With such restrictions, the asset allocations are conservative. As of June 2009, 91.4 percent of DB plan assets and 64.8 percent of DC plan assets were invested in instruments with guaranteed principal.[38]

In China, DC plan participants are not allowed to direct their investments. The authority to make investment-related decisions lies with the institution designated as trustee, which could be either a corporate pension board composed of representatives of the company and employees or a specialized institution with trustee credentials, such as a trust investment company or insurance company.[39] When a corporate pension board is the trustee, usually both labor and management are members of the institution that makes high-level investment-related decisions. That is similar to the arrangement with collective DC plans in the Netherlands. One problem with collective investment in DC plans is that employees bear the investment risk but lack the authority to make investment decisions. That can be alleviated somewhat by putting employee representatives on the governing board, but it still does not overcome the difficulty of shoehorning participants of different ages and with different risk tolerances into the same investments.

Japan also used to restrict the asset allocations of DB plans. The old 5:3:3:2 rule, which was phased out in the 1990s, required at least a 50 percent allocation to safe assets, no more than a 30 percent allocation to stocks and to foreign currency-denominated assets, and no more than a 20 percent allocation to real estate. The DC plans introduced in 2001 started out without any asset allocation restrictions, although they were required to provide at least one product in the principal-secured category, which includes deposit accounts and insurance products with a guaranteed yield. According to the Japan Association of DC Plan Administrators, as of March 2009, 67.4 percent of DC plan assets were invested

37. OECD (2010).

38. Data from Korea Financial Supervisory Service, "Korea's Retirement Pension Market in H1 2009 and Future Prospects," press release, September 8, 2009.

39. Asset allocation is restricted to at least 20 percent for deposit-like products (deposits and money market funds), 50 percent for fixed-income products (including CDs, government bonds, corporate bonds, and bond funds), 30 percent for equities (stocks, equity funds, and investment-like insurance products), and less than 20 percent for individual equities.

in principal-secured products (45.1 percent in deposits and 22.3 percent in insurance) and 32.5 percent were invested in investment trusts and others. That is a fairly conservative allocation in light of the age distribution of plan participants, 19 percent of whom are in their twenties, 33 percent in their thirties, 30 percent in their forties, and 17 percent in their fifties.[40]

Although DC investment continues to be an issue for debate, probably a bigger source of the inadequacy of Japan's DC plans is the low maximum contribution and the inability of plan participants to contribute to corporate DC plans. Legislation proposing that participants be allowed to make contributions has recently been submitted to the Diet. That is a reform that needs to be implemented promptly, given that the system is posited as one based on individual responsibility. The fundamental reason behind the difficulty in introducing participant contributions or raising contribution limits is the view that tax incentives for enhancing household saving rates are unnecessary. However, now that attention is often called to the rapid decrease in Japan's savings rate, it is likely that such views need to be revised.

All three countries therefore have room for improvement in their corporate pension systems, on both the contribution and investment sides. The issue for China is whether to continue with the collective investment approach or to allow individuals to make their own investment decisions. The question in Korea is whether investment restrictions should remain in place for corporate pensions, which were introduced five years ago. In Japan, in addition to allowing employee contributions, the maximum contribution needs to be raised so that DC plans are capable of building sufficient assets. On the investment side, given that Japan's DC plans are based on the U.S. model, there probably is need for debate on how to position investments in the default product.[41]

Conclusion

This chapter looks at pension reforms in Japan, Korea, and China in the context of global trends in pension reform, which can be characterized as a shift from public pensions to private pensions, an increase in levels of prefunding, and a shift from DB plans to DC plans (table 2-5).

Of the three major trends, all three countries are raising the level of prefunding by establishing and managing public pension reserve funds. Japan has the world's largest public pension reserve fund, and both Korea and China are rapidly

40. Data from Unei Kanri Kikan Renraku Kyogikai (Japan Association of DC Plan Administrators), "Kakutei Kyoshutu Nenkin Tokei Shiryo" [DC Statistical Material].

41. Currently, investment in default products is considered a stopgap measure used only until the participant gives investment instructions. Deposits typically are designated as the default product.

Table 2-5. *Global Trends in Pension Reform and Conditions in Japan, Korea, and China*

Trend	Japan	Korea	China
Shift from public pensions to private pensions	Public pension reform of 2004 lowered replacement rate, but the maximum contribution to DC plans was raised only slightly. Private pension funds as a percentage of GDP are only one-third the OECD average.	The replacement rate is being incrementally lowered. A minimum pension has been introduced. Corporate pensions were introduced in 2005; roughly 20 percent of those eligible enroll.	The coverage rate of the public pension only 20 percent, well below the OECD average of 83 percent; raising the rate is a priority.
Increasing levels of prefunding	The GPIF is the world's largest pension fund. Fund's investments focus on domestic bonds.	National Pension Fund, established in 1999, is now growing rapidly. The fund invests in overseas real estate, infrastructure, and other alternative investments.	Funded individual accounts were introduced into the public pension system. The National Social Security Fund was established in 2000 to provide future surplus funds.
Shift from DB to DC plans	Defined contribution plans were introduced in 2001. The number of participants is growing but still is substantially smaller than the number in defined benefit plans; assets also remain small.	Introduced both DB and DC plans in 2005. Larger firms appear to be using DB plans.	Only defined contribution–type plans are allowed for new corporate pension plans.

Source: Nomura Institute of Capital Markets Research.

building their own reserves. In addition, Korea has been aggressively adding alternative investments to its portfolio. In the area of governance structures, however, all three countries have room for improvement in terms of the independence of their pension systems from the government.

Both Japan and Korea have begun lowering the replacement rate and reducing the role of their public pensions in providing retirement income. To fill the gap, Korea introduced corporate pensions in 2005, and more time is needed to judge whether a shift from public to private pensions is truly under way. Meanwhile, Japan's public pension reforms of 2004 set in motion a lowering of the replacement rate but only slightly increased the maximum contribution to DC plans in a weak attempt to strengthen private pensions. Japan faces the most difficult pension system environment of the three countries, namely huge government deficits and a rapidly aging population. Improving the sustainability of the public pension should be a priority, and it would be reasonable to rely on private pensions for adequacy of benefits. Japan needs to clearly delineate the respective roles of its public and private pension systems.

While in China new corporate pension plans must be DC plans, Japan and Korea allow companies to choose between DB and DC plans. There has yet to be any clear shift from DB plans to DC plans. Although it has been almost nine years since Japan introduced DC plans, only 3.4 million, or 10 percent, of private sector employees have enrolled, and DB plans are still considerably larger. Korea introduced both DB and DC corporate pensions at the same time, and although a larger number of companies offer the latter, DB plans exceed DC plans in both number of participants and total assets.

The basic direction of pension reform in Japan, Korea, and China aligns with the global trend. Each country has its own set of challenges, however, and it will be interesting to see how they will overcome them. Although Japan may be slightly ahead of the other two countries in terms of the timing of the introduction of pension schemes, all three are in a position to learn from the U.S. and European experiences. As the three countries leverage their position moving forward, it will be interesting to see whether a solution originates in Asia when the next global trends develop, such as the search for a way to guarantee lifetime income through DC pensions.

References

Ambachtsheer, Keith. 2007. *Pension Revolution: A Solution to the Pensions Crisis.* John Wiley and Sons.

European Federation for Retirement Provision (EFRP). 2010. "Workplace Pensions: Defined Contribution." March.

Holzmann, Robert, and Richard Hinz. 2005. *Old-Age Income Support in the 21st Century: An International Perspective on Pension Systems and Reform*. World Bank.

Japan Ministry of Health, Labor, and Welfare. 2005. *Kosei Nenkin/Kokumin Nenkin–Heisei 16 Nen Zaisei Saikeisan Kekka* [Results of Recalculating 2004 Finances of Employee and National Pensions].

———. 2010. "Nenkin Tsumitatekin Kanri Unyo Dokuritsu Gyosei Hojinno Uneino Arikatani Kansuru Kentokai Hokoku" [Final Report of Study Group on GPIF Management]. December.

Nomura, Akiko. 2006. "Beikokuno Kigyo Nenkin Kaikakuho nit suite" [U.S. Corporate Pension Reform]. *Nomura Shihon Shijo Quarterly*. Fall.

———. 2008. "Koutekinenkin Setsuritsukin Unyou no Gabanansu wo Meguru Giron" [Debating Governance of Investments by Public Pension Reserve Funds]. *Zaikai Kansoku*. October.

———. 2009a. "Proposal for Fundamentally Reforming Japan's Defined Contribution Pensions." *Nomura Journal of Capital Markets* 1, no. 3 (November 19).

———. 2009b. "Kinyu Kikiwo Hete Kakuteikyoshutugata Nenkin Kakujuwo Mezasu Beikoku Obama Seiken" [Obama Administration's Policy to Enhance Defined Contribution Plans after Financial Crisis]. *Nomura Shihon Shijo Quarterly*. Fall.

Nomura Institute of Capital Markets Research. 2007. *Chugoku Shouken Shijou Taizen* [All about the Chinese Securities Market]. Nihon Keizai Shimbun-sha.

Ono, Masaaki. 2007. "Fuka Houshiki ni yoru Kouteki Nenkin Seido no Un'ei ni okeru Setsuritsu Suijun no arikata" [Reserve Funds for Operating PAYGO Public Pensions]. *Kaigai Shakai Hosho Kenkyuu* [Research on Social Security Overseas]. Spring.

Organization for Economic Cooperation and Development (OECD). 2009. *Pensions at a Glance 2009: Retirement Income Systems in OECD Countries* (www.oecd.org/els/social/pensions/PAG).

———. 2007. *Pensions at a Glance 2007: Public Policies across OECD Countries*.

———. 2010. "Survey of Investment Regulation of Pension Funds." February (www.oecd.org/dataoecd/53/43/44679793.pdf).

Park, Jung-bae. 2009. "Kankoku Nenkin Seido no Doukou" [Trends in Korea's Pension Systems]. *Kaigai Shakai Hosho Kenkyuu* [Research on Social Security Overseas]. Summer.

Ryu, Jae-kwang. 2010. "Kankoku no Taishoku Kyuufu Seido no Genjou to Kadai" [On the Korean Retirement Pension Plan]. *Nenkin to Keizai* [Pensions and the Economy] 28, no. 4 (January).

Sekine, Eiichi. 2009. "Chugoku no Koutekinenkin Unyou" [The Investment of China's Pension Fund]. *Nenkin to Keizai* [Pensions and the Economy] 28, no. 1 (April).

Sekine, Eiichi, and Nomura, Akiko. 2009. Zhongguo gonggong yanglao chubeijin yunzuo zhili fangshi [Governance of Chinese Public Pension Reserve Management]. October (www.nicmr.com/nicmr/chinese/report/repo/2009/200910_01.pdf).

United Nations. 2009. World Population Prospects: The 2008 Revision Population Database. (http://esa.un.org/unpd/wpp2008/index.htm).

ROBERT NOVY-MARX
JOSHUA RAUH

3

The Crisis in Local Government Pensions in the United States

S TATE AND LOCAL GOVERNMENTS follow the same accounting framework for measuring the value of their pension promises. The value of those promises is disclosed in accordance with Government Accounting Standards Board (GASB) statement 25, which stipulates that benefit promises are to be discounted at an assumed return on pension plan assets. That assumed return determines how the future stream of cash benefits that the state or local government has promised is converted into a present value liability measure. It also governs the actuarial recommendation for the annual amount that state and local governments set aside to fund newly promised benefits. The higher the assumed return, the lower the present value of recognized benefit cash flows and the less money the government entity sets aside on a flow basis to cover a given benefit stream.

As we have pointed out previously (Novy-Marx and Rauh 2009, 2010a, and 2010b), this system misrepresents the value of pension promises. The field of financial economics is unified in agreeing that the present value of a stream of cash flows is a function of the risk of the cash flows themselves. The pension payments promised to government workers do not depend on the performance of pension fund assets. The value of the liability therefore depends on the risk

We are grateful to Olivia Mitchell and conference participants for comments and discussions. We thank Suzanne Chang and Kevin Soter for research assistance.

of the stream of cash flows associated with that liability, not on the assets that back the liability.

If households could use the GASB accounting system, then they could write down the value of their mortgages by simply reallocating their savings from a money market account to the stock market. By doing so, they would increase the expected rate of return on their assets and get to use that higher rate to discount their debts. If state and local governments took further advantage of this system, they could make their liabilities essentially disappear by taking on risky investments with high average returns and high risk.

In previous work we have shown that the total liability for the major pension plans sponsored by the fifty U.S. state governments is approximately $5 trillion using Treasury discount rates, contrary to government accounting, which would point to total liabilities of only $3 trillion. The unfunded liability for the major pension plans sponsored by the fifty U.S. state governments is approximately $3 trillion using Treasury discount rates, contrary to government accounting, which would point to unfunded liabilities of only $1 trillion.

In this chapter, we examine municipal pension promises. In particular, we apply financial valuation to seventy-seven pension plans sponsored by fifty major cities, counties, and other local government entities. This sample represents all nonstate municipal entities with more than $1 billion in pension assets, covering 2.04 million local public employees and retirees. According to the U.S. Census of Governments, a total of 3.03 million individuals is covered by 2,332 local pension plans in the United States.[1] Thus, while we capture only 3 percent of municipal pension plans, we capture about two-thirds of the universe of municipal workers.

According to the latest reports issued by the local governments themselves, they have $488 billion in liabilities. When we reverse-engineer the cash flows and limit recognition to only those benefits that have been promised based on today's service and salary and use the plan-chosen discount rates, that figure drops to $430 billion. When we use taxable AA+ municipal yield curves to discount those benefits, we obtain liability measures that are around 18 percent larger. When we use the Treasury yield curve, we find a total liability of $681 billion, which is 39 percent above the stated level and 58 percent above the already promised benefit at municipally chosen rates. Net of the assets in the plans, the unfunded liability is $383 billion using Treasury discounting, or over $5,300 per capita and over $185,000 per member. If on a per-member basis the unfunded liability is the same for the approximately 1 million local workers covered by municipal plans

---

1. See the 2008 survey of State and Local Government Employee Retirement Systems (U.S. Census Bureau 2008).

not in our sample, the total unfunded liability for all municipal plans in the United States is $574 billion.[2]

The method of discounting using municipal yield curves credits cities that experience rating downgrades with lower liabilities. If local taxpayers can default on pensions in the same circumstances that they can default on bonds, then muni discounting would represent the city's exposure. However, given the legal protections that exist for state and local government pensions in many states— as well as the political reality that in past municipal crises the pensions have been paid while the localities' bonds have been impaired—a better measure of overall taxpayer liability is obtained by treating accrued pension benefits as a default-free promise and by discounting using Treasury yields.

For the states, implementing Treasury discount rates increases total liabilities by around 66 percent, whereas in the municipalities that we study the impact is smaller, at 39 percent. This reflects the fact that the retired member share in the municipal plans averages 43 percent, while the retired member share in the state plans averages only 36 percent. As a result, the municipal plans have shorter duration than the state plans and are less affected by the correction of the discount rates.

The $0.6 trillion unfunded liability in major municipalities obviously is much smaller than a $3 trillion unfunded liability for state governments. Relative to the municipalities' resources and taxes, however, the unfunded liability is substantial. The fifty municipalities with the $382 billion unfunded liability that we measure had 2006 revenues of $120 billion. The unfunded liability is therefore equivalent to 3.2 years of revenue. For the comparable time period, the 116 state-sponsored plans had a $2.52 trillion unfunded liability and $0.78 trillion in revenues, for a ratio of 3.2 years of revenue. Thus, relative to current tax resources, the extent of the gap between assets and liabilities in the municipal plans is almost exactly the same as in state plans.

In this chapter we first present the sample and our calculations of municipal pension liabilities under current reporting. We then review the different methods of recognizing accruals and the arguments about appropriate discount rates. Next we present our model for translating among liability concepts and for calculating municipal pension liabilities using different yield curves. Following that we describe the present value calculations under alternative yield curves and calculate the number of years that the existing assets of each municipality could pay benefits at currently promised levels. We close with a summary and our conclusions.

2. Since we used an asset cutoff in selecting the sample, the unfunded liability on a per-member basis is in fact likely to be somewhat larger for the plans not in our sample than for the plans in our sample.

Sample and Municipal Pension Obligations
under Current Reporting

The sample consists of seventy-seven defined benefit pension systems sponsored by local governments. The sample was identified using detailed 2006 data from the U.S. Census of Governments. We first selected all plans with more than $1 billion in assets as of 2006, the latest year for which the detailed census of state and local government retirement systems was available. That amounted to seventy-eight plans. We then added any other plans sponsored by the same local government entities with at least $100 million in assets, for a total of ninety plans, to ensure that for any of the municipalities in our sample, all substantive pension plans would be counted.[3] We then constructed a unique dataset by searching the local government websites for the Comprehensive Annual Financial Report (CAFR) for each of the plans. Due to data availability issues, we were forced to discard the plans from several major municipalities including Denver (Colorado), Austin (Texas), and Minneapolis (Minnesota).

The final sample encompasses seventy-seven pension systems in fifty major municipalities. The census of governments classifies each plan according to the type of local entity that sponsors the plan. Twenty-eight of the seventy-seven systems are sponsored by county governments, and forty-five are sponsored by city governments. Of the remaining four plans, two (the Chicago Teachers' Pension Fund and the St. Paul Teachers' Association Retirement Fund) are sponsored by school districts that are coterminous with cities but may receive funding from a variety of sources. The last two plans are Chicago plans sponsored by special districts—the water district and the Chicago Transit Authority—which also receive funding from a variety of sources. To the extent that there is substantial overlap between the taxpayers of the school districts or special districts and the municipalities with which they overlap, we combine the pension funds of these entities with any local municipal systems that may exist.

Table 3-1 presents summary statistics on the membership of the seventy-seven systems as well as membership data for the ten plans that are largest in total membership. There are 2.04 million workers in these plans; according to the U.S. Census of Governments, a total of 3.03 million total workers is covered by all local government pension plans. On average, 53 percent of the workers in the sample plans are current employees. Systems that have a larger share of active workers will face larger benefit cash flows further in the future and the duration of their cash flows will be longer.

---

3. There were 277 total plans with more than $100 million in assets as of 2006.

Table 3-1. *Summary of Plans and Participants*[a]

| | Number of members | | | | |
Summary and plans	Active	Annuitant	Separated and vested	Total	Active (percent)
Summary statistic					
Total	1,109,095	809,214	122,944	2,042,253	54
Mean	14,404	10,496	1,597	26,497	53
Median	6,277	5,322	595	11,810	53
Standard deviation	26,675	18,363	2,581	46,840	8
Ten largest plans					
New York City Employee Retirement System	187,327	133,277	8,949	329,554	57
Teachers' Retirement System of the City of New York	114,307	71,259	6,247	191,812	60
Los Angeles County Employees' Retirement System	96,382	53,397	12,071	161,850	60
New York City Police Pension Fund	36,044	45,176	829	82,049	44
Municipal Employees' Annuity and Benefit Fund of Chicago	33,214	23,185	12,324	68,723	48
City of Philadelphia Municipal Retirement System	28,632	35,694	1,336	65,662	44
Chicago Teachers' Pension Fund	32,728	24,398	3,549	60,675	54
San Francisco Employees' Retirement System	31,263	21,944	4,841	58,048	54
Boston Retirement System	22,512	14,408	9,896	46,817	48

Source: Authors' calculations based on the Comprehensive Annual Financial Report for each of seventy-seven plans.

a. The top panel summarizes the number of individual members in each of three main categories: active workers, annuitants, and those who are vested but no longer in public employment. The sample includes seventy-seven major city- and county-sponsored pension plans, covering two-thirds of the universe of workers in municipal pension systems. All major plans in fifty major municipal systems are represented. The bottom panel lists these data for the ten state-sponsored pension plans that are the largest by total number of members.

Each municipality reports a measure of total liabilities in the CAFR. A starting point for total liabilities would be simply to take a raw sum of liabilities from the reports, which yields a total of $464 billion. However, the date of the latest available CAFR is not the same for each system, so the liabilities must be harmonized to a June 2009 reporting date.[4] Assuming a 7 percent benefit growth rate (which actually is conservative relative to the rate at which stated benefits have been growing), we arrive at total liabilities of $488 billion as of June 2009 on a stated basis.

Rediscounting of cash flows under different actuarial accrual concepts and different yield curves requires an estimate of the cash flows themselves. Unfortunately, the local governments do not provide the cash flows that they use to derive the liabilities that they report. To derive estimates of cash flow streams based on the information provided in the CAFRs therefore requires using a calibrated model and making a series of assumptions. We explain the calibration itself later in the chapter.

Accrual Methods and Discount Rates

Most estimates of liabilities that are not conducted by economists simply add up the liabilities that are disclosed in the CAFRs. That method ignores two issues. First, it relies strictly on the liability concept that state actuaries choose without considering what liabilities are actually being recognized. Second, adding liabilities disclosed in the CAFRs takes as given whatever discount rate the state actuaries have chosen.

Liability Concepts

We consider four different liability concepts: accumulated benefit obligation (ABO), projected benefit obligation (PBO), entry age normal (EAN), and projected value of benefits (PVB). The narrowest measure is the ABO, which reflects benefits already promised and accrued. In other words, even if a pension plan could be completely frozen, the city would still contractually owe those benefits. The ABO is not affected by uncertainty about future wages and service, as the cash flows associated with the ABO are based on information known today: plan benefit formulas, current salaries, and current years of service. One source of uncertainty in the ABO is inflation, in particular the magnitude of cost of living

---

4. The distribution of latest reporting dates is as follows: June 2007 (1), September 2007 (1), December 2007 (3), June 2008 (23), September 2008 (5), December 2008 (17), June 2009 (22), September 2009 (2), December 2009 (3).

adjustments (COLAs) in cities where such adjustments are linked to official statistics such as CPI inflation.

The ABO is often thought of as a "termination liability"—that is, the liability that would be owed today even if plans were frozen completely or all workers were fired. In fact, the ABO actually could be somewhat less than a termination liability, as it assumes that an employee does not start taking benefits until his retirement date, which might be later than the full retirement age. A termination liability assumes that employees take benefits at the earliest advantageous date, which typically is earlier than the full retirement age given the fact that actuarial adjustments for early retirement are generally less than actuarially fair.

If workers receive their marginal product in total compensation (wages plus pension benefits), the ABO is the only concept that should be considered since it measures the benefits that employees have actually earned (Bulow 1982; Brown and Wilcox 2009). The ABO is a "narrow" measure in that it does not recognize any future wage increases or future service that employees are expected to provide, even though such increases and service are to some extent predictable. Moreover, the ABO obligation is independent of wage risk, which simplifies the valuation.

The three broader measures (PBO, EAN, and PVB) all account to varying extents for the fact that benefits continue to accrue due to the future salary and/or service of existing workers. They assume that the pension system will not be frozen today, and they all aim to reflect some portion of actual expected benefits.

The broadest measure, the PVB, represents a discounted present value of the full projection of the cash flows that actuaries expect the city to owe. The PVB method does not credit the government for the fact that it might have some ability to limit benefit accruals. Both the EAN and the PBO recognize a fraction of the PVB; therefore they are intermediate measures between the ABO and the PVB.

The PBO accounts fully for expected future wage increases for existing workers but not expected future service. Mathematically, the PBO formula recognizes the PVB in a way that is prorated by service. Note that Financial Accounting Standards Board (FASB) accounting for publicly traded corporations requires the calculation of a PBO.

The EAN is broader than the PBO but not as broad as the PVB. Mathematically, the EAN method recognizes the PVB in proportion to discounted wages earned to date relative to discounted expected lifetime wages. In practice, this procedure accounts for some portion of future benefit accruals due to both future wages and future service.

Table 3-2 summarizes the liability concepts. Further details, including formulas, are provided in Novy-Marx and Rauh (2010a). We note that none of these

Table 3-2. *Description of Methods for Recognizing Accrued Liabilities*[a]

Method	Broadness
Accumulated benefit obligation (ABO)	Represents promised benefits under current salary and years of service. Often used inter-changeably with the concept of "termination liability," or liability if the plan were frozen, although there are some differences (see text).
Projected benefit obligation (PBO)	Takes projected future salary increases but not future years of service into account in calculating today's liability. Used in FASB accounting for corporations.
Entry age normal (EAN)	Reflects a portion of future salary and service by allowing new liabilities to accrue as a fixed percentage of a worker's salary throughout his or her career.
Present value of benefits (PVB)	Presents a full projection of what current employees are expected to be owed if their salary grows and they work and retire according to actuarial assumptions.

Source: Authors' compilation.

a. The table summarizes the four main methods for recognizing pension liabilities. The methods differ in their treatment of expected future salary increases and service that is yet to be performed. The methods are listed in increasing order of broadness, starting with the method that reflects only current service and salary and ending with the method that reflects a full projection of benefits that are expected to be paid.

methods account for the expected benefits that will be owed to workers who have not yet been hired.

Discount Rates

As explained in Novy-Marx and Rauh (2009; 2010a), the discount rate that state and local governments use under GASB accounting procedures does not reflect the risk of the liabilities. Discounting liabilities at an expected rate of return on the assets in the plan runs counter to the entire logic of financial economics: financial streams of payment should be discounted at a rate that reflects their risk (Modigliani and Miller 1958), in particular their covariance with priced risks (Treynor 1961; Sharpe 1964; Lintner 1965).

Governments discount the liabilities at a flat rate, and usually that rate is very close to 8 percent. As shown in table 3-3, the mean discount rate for the seventy-seven systems in our sample is 8.03 percent, the median rate is 8.00 percent,

Table 3-3. *Discount Rates Used by Municipal Plans*
Percent

Mean	8.03
Median	8.00
Standard deviation	0.36
Minimum	7.50
Maximum	10.00
Number of plans	77

Source: Authors' calculations based on the Comprehensive Annual Financial Report for each of seventy-seven plans.

and the standard deviation is 0.36 percent. The model rate is 8.00 percent, used by thirty-three of the seventy-seven systems. Governments justify their discount rates with the argument that they are discounting liabilities at the expected rate of return on the assets in their pension fund. Such a procedure ignores the risk of the assets completely and treats returns above the risk-free rate as a free lunch.

The GASB procedures have survived criticism in part because observers have noted that many pension systems have earned average returns of around 8 percent over the past decades. But again, that assumes that the 8 percent was obtained without any risk. In fact, those returns were obtained by taking investment risk, and if the assets had not returned 8 percent, taxpayers would have been on the hook for additional shortfalls. If systems want to be able to tell their employees that the benefit stream is safer than a portfolio of stocks and bonds, they should discount the cash flows in a way that reflects that safety.

Novy-Marx and Rauh (2010a) employs two primary discounting procedures. The first uses the taxable muni rate, defined as the local municipal yield grossed up for a tax preference on muni debt, assuming a 25 percent marginal rate for the marginal municipal bond holder (Poterba and Verdugo 2008). The second method uses the Treasury yield curve.

Using the muni rate admits and quantifies a probability of default. The liability is a measure that calculates the present value of the defaultable liability from the perspective of the taxpayers under the assumption that the municipalities will default on those payments in the same states of the world as those in which they would default on their general obligation (GO) debt, and with the same recovery rates. Alternatively, it is the value of the portfolio of local GO bonds that the municipalities would need to deliver to the plan to defease the obligation. When assessing the difference in the liability under different policy measures, the comparative statics quantify the size of the shift in the value of those uncertain payments.

Discounting a liability at the taxable muni rate captures some of the spirit of the FASB rules for corporate pension discounting. The FASB rules let corporations discount pension obligations at high-grade corporate bond rates. Discounting local pension obligations at municipal bond rates is similar in that the creditworthiness of the asset class (municipal or corporate bonds) plays a role. In this chapter, we assume that the AA+ yield curve would be appropriate for all municipalities under this procedure.[5]

Crediting governments by reducing pension liabilities based on GO default premiums leads if anything to understatement of the liability to the taxpayer. Most important, benefits often are given special protections in state constitutions as well as in statutory and common law (Brown and Wilcox 2009). The priority accorded to public pension cash flows suggests that they should be discounted at rates lower than the GO bond yield. In most local government situations, a pension default is less likely than a GO debt default (consider Vallejo, California). Even if cities were to default on pension promises, pension obligations might well have a higher recovery rate than GO debt. Somewhat offsetting the limitations on municipal pension defaults is the possibility that municipalities might receive a bailout from the state or federal government for pension promises (consider Harrisburg, Pennsylvania, for example), in which case taxpayers of a given city might view the pension liabilities as less certainly owed by them. However, because our focus is on an aggregate liability calculation across municipalities, this issue would affect the distribution of liabilities across cities and states but not the total liability to all U.S. taxpayers.

Using the Treasury yield curve values the pension benefits as secure promises. The Treasury valuations start from the premise that the benefits will be paid. To the extent that they are not paid, there is a transfer from participants to tax-payers. The expected value of the transfers would reduce the value of the payments to the participants but also reduce the cost to the taxpayer. Treasury discounting can therefore be viewed as valuing the benefits as a default-free promise. If local pension systems want to present to their employees the idea that the benefits are default free, they must discount at default-free rates. If a local pension system wanted to contract out the provision of the benefits to an insurer that would

5. There are some additional important differences. First, FASB rules require firms to recognize the PBO, whereas our primary focus is on the ABO. Second, a firm will owe little beyond the assets in the pension fund if the firm becomes insolvent, since the Pension Benefit Guaranty Corporation (PBGC) will take over the plan and become an unsecured creditor in bankruptcy. States are not insured by the PBGC, and even if the state defaults on its debt, there is a high likelihood that it will have to pay pensions.

make the benefit payments even if in the future the municipality defaulted on some of its obligations, the insurance company would presumably value the liability at a default-free rate.

There are important caveats about using the Treasury yield curve as a measure of risk in a default-free pension liability. Although the Treasury yield curve is generally viewed as default free, it reflects other risks that may not be present in the pension liability. State employee pensions typically contain COLAs. If inflation risk is priced (Fisher 1975; Barro 1976), then an appropriate default-free pension discount rate would involve a downward adjustment of nominal yields to remove the inflation risk premium. That adjustment would further increase the present value of ABO liabilities. However, a countervailing factor is the fact that Treasuries trade at a premium due to their liquidity (Woodford 1990; Duffie and Singleton 1997; Longstaff 2004; Krishnamurthy and Vissing-Jorgensen 2008). Pension obligations are nowhere near as liquid as Treasuries. Therefore a liquidity price premium should ideally be removed from Treasury rates before using them to discount default-free but illiquid obligations.

Given the lack of consensus over the relative size of the liquidity price premium and inflation yield premium, we use unadjusted Treasury rates to calculate our default-free liability measures. However, we note that due to the factors priced into the Treasury curve, default-free public pension obligations are not equivalent to Treasuries.[6]

Calculating Liabilities under Different Accrual Concepts and Discount Rates

Novy-Marx and Rauh (2010a), which considers state plans, provides a detailed account of our methodology. The basic challenge is that plans are discounting cash flows using a simple discounted cash flow formula:

$$L_{i,\text{stated}} = \sum_{t=1}^{T} \frac{C_{i,t}}{\left(1 + r_{i,\text{stated}}\right)^{t'}}.$$

However, plans do not report the cash flows $(C_{i,t})$, which appear in the numerator.

Our model delivers a forecast of each plan's cash flow each year in the future under the different accrual concepts. The model uses plan-level information

---

6. Novy-Marx and Rauh (2010a) also note that if wages are correlated with the stock market over long horizons, some correction for that correlation might be useful in the discount factor, but only for the broader measures. The ABO is independent of future wage growth.

regarding the number of active, retired, and separated workers as well as the benefit factor (that is, the fraction of salary that, when multiplied by years of service, determines a participant's initial benefit), cost of living adjustment, and inflation assumption employed by the plan. We collected that information individually from the CAFRs. The calculation also employs assumptions regarding the relative number of employees and average wages by age and years of service (an "age-service matrix"); salary growth and separation probabilities by age; and the relative number of annuitants and average level of benefits for annuitants of each age.

The benefit calculations assume that the full retirement age is sixty and that a younger retiree can start taking benefits up to five years early by incurring a linear 6 percent benefit reduction for each year that he or she retires before age sixty. The calculation also requires the average salary of the working plan members, which we estimate as $65,182 in 2009.

We project benefits by assuming mortality rates from the RP-2000 tables (Society of Actuaries 2000), which are employed by many state and local governments. We use the tables' combined (employee/retired) healthy rates and assume that participants are evenly divided by gender, that 60 percent are married to a spouse of the same age at the time that they retire, and that plans allow for 50 percent survivor benefits.

We then calibrate each plan's cash flows by adjusting the average salary of the employed and the average benefits of the non-active members. They are calibrated to simultaneously match both the plan's stated accounting liability when capitalized at the city-chosen discount rate using the actuarial method employed by the city and the plan's expected first-year cash flow, which we estimate at 107 percent of the cash flow for the year ending June 2009, based on recent historical cash flow growth.

Some of these calculations require additional data, which we explain here, reflecting assumptions about salaries, years of service, and wages. In particular, we need the distribution of plan participants by age and years of service (age-service matrix) and the average wages of employees in each cell. For that purpose we use the representative average age-service matrix of public plans used in Novy-Marx and Rauh (2010a).[7] We also require salary growth and separation probabilities, by age, for active workers, vectors that also come from Novy-Marx and Rauh (2010a).

---

7. That matrix was based on selecting the ten states with the largest total liabilities and then searching the CAFRs for age-service matrices. The age-service matrices were available for New York, Illinois, Pennsylvania, Ohio, and Texas. While this is the age-service matrix for workers in state-sponsored plans, we expect the age-service profile of local plans to be similar.

Table 3-4. *Distribution of Retirees and Average Annuity, by Age*[a]

Age bracket	Percent of retirees	Average annuity (dollars)
Under 50	5	22,568
50–54	6	33,457
55–59	11	38,092
60–64	19	37,020
65–69	17	31,908
70–74	14	27,685
75–79	11	25,684
80–84	9	23,159
85–89	5	20,045
90+	3	17,440
Total	100	30,091

Source: Authors' calculations based on the seventeen Comprehensive Annual Financial Reports mentioned above.

a. The Comprehensive Annual Financial Report for each of the seventy-seven sample plans was searched for distribution of retirees and average annuity by age. That information was provided in seventeen plans: Anne Arundel County Retirement System, Baltimore Employees' Retirement System, City of Philadelphia Municipal Retirement System, Fire and Police Employees' Retirement System of Baltimore, Laborers' and Retirement Board Employees' Annuity and Benefit Fund of Chicago, Metropolitan Water Reclamation District Fund of Greater Chicago, New York City Board of Education Retirement System, New York City Employee Retirement System, New York City Fire Pension Fund, New York City Police Pension Fund, Retirement Plan for Chicago Transit Authority Employees, Retirement System for Employees of the City of Cincinnati, San Joaquin County Employees' Retirement Association, Santa Barbara County Employees' Retirement System, Seattle City Employees' Retirement System, Tacoma Employees' Retirement System, and Teachers' Retirement System of the City of New York. The statistics here represent equal-weighted averages across those plans.

For retired workers, we employ a distribution of retirees by age and the average annuity benefit in each age category. That information is only sporadically disclosed, but by sampling the local CAFRs we obtained an average distribution across seventeen plans covering 274,063 of the 808,214 annuitants in our sample plans. Table 3-4 shows the average fraction of retirees and average annuity in each age group, and the note to the table lists the plans from which the distribution was derived. Over 40 percent of the retirees are under age sixty-five. The average annuity is highest for fifty-five- to fifty-nine-year-olds, at over $38,000, and lowest for the oldest retirees, who presumably retired under less generous benefit regimes. The overall average annuity is $30,000.

The total cash flows delivered by the model are illustrated in figure 3-1. By construction, discounting the dashed line (EAN) in the figure at 8 percent yields a number very close to the stated liability (the only difference being that a few

Figure 3-1. *Projected Aggregate Cash Flows for Seventy-Seven Major Municipal Pension Systems*[a]

Billions of dollars

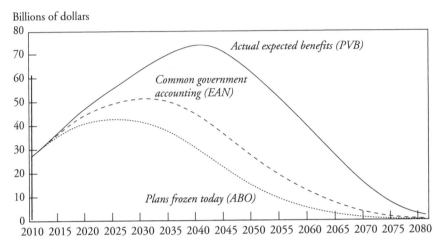

Source: Authors' calculations based on our model and inputs from seventy-seven Comprehensive Annual Financial Reports.

a. This figure shows projected aggregate local government cash flows under different accrual methods given public pension promises. Cash flow projections for each local plan are made so that the plan's reported liability equals the discounted value of the cash flow under the municipality's chosen accrual method and reported discount rate.

plans use a method different from the EAN). The solid line shows what would happen to total cash flows across the seventy-seven municipalities if all the plans were frozen today. The benefits would peak at around $42 billion annually in 2025. If plans are not frozen, however, the top line is the best estimate of what actual benefits will be, peaking at over $70 billion around the year 2040. That peak occurs slightly later than the peak calculated for state defined benefit pension plans calculated in Novy-Marx and Rauh (2010a), primarily because retired municipal workers are younger than retired state workers.[8]

Figure 3-2 breaks the benefits down into cash flows owed to currently active employees (panel A) and to currently retired employees and the remainder, who currently are neither in public employment nor drawing a pension but are entitled to draw a pension at some future date (panel B). The liability due to current annuitants and separated workers is insensitive to the accrual method,

8. For example, while in our sample 11 percent of retired municipal workers are under fifty-five, that is true for only 3.5 percent of retired state workers in Novy-Marx and Rauh (2010a).

Figure 3-2. *Projected Aggregate Cash Flows for Active, Annuitant, and Separated Participants*

Billions of dollars

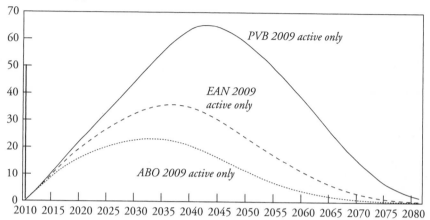

Billions of dollars

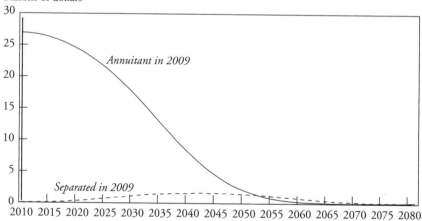

Source: Authors' calculations based on our model and inputs from seventy-seven Comprehensive Annual Financial Reports.

Figure 3-3. *Zero-Coupon Yield Curves as of June 30, 2009*[a]

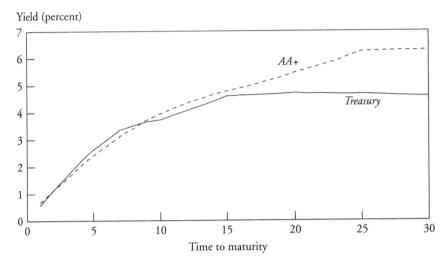

Yield (percent)

Time to maturity

Source: Underlying data were downloaded from the Bloomberg YCRV screen.

a. This graph shows zero-coupon yield curves for Treasuries as well as AA+ municipal bonds as of June 30, 2009. Yields on coupon bonds were collected from Bloomberg. The zero-coupon yields were calculated from strip prices, which we obtained by constructing long-short portfolios of the coupon bonds.

since the accrual method is a question of how to treat future wage growth service by the employees who are currently in active employment.

The Present Value of Pension Promises

Figure 3-3 shows the alternative discount rates that we apply. This graph shows zero-coupon yield curves for Treasuries as well as AA+ municipal bonds as of June 30, 2009. Yields on coupon bonds were collected from Bloomberg. The zero-coupon yields were calculated from strip prices, which we obtained by constructing long-short portfolios of the coupon bonds.

Table 3-5 shows the present value of municipal liabilities under the different methods. The first cell in the upper left represents the raw sum of liabilities on an as-reported basis harmonized to June 2009. As explained previously, this starting point for the liability is $488 billion. The other figures in the left column of the table show the sensitivity of the liability to the use of different accrual methods while retaining the municipally chosen discount rate. Moving from the municipally chosen method, which is usually the EAN, to the ABO reduces the liability to $430 billion. Moving to the expansive PVB results in a liability of $581 billion.

Table 3-5. *Municipal Liabilities under Different Discount Rates and Actuarial Methods*
Billions of dollars

| | Discount rate | | |
Participant type and method	Municipal-chosen	Taxable muni	Treasury
Total participants (active + annuitant + separated)			
As stated, unharmonized	$488		
Accumulated benefit obligation (ABO)	430	507	681
Projected benefit obligation (PBO)	477	557	784
Entry age normal (EAN)	489	571	810
Projected value of benefits (PVB)	581	662	1.047
Active participants only			
Accumulated benefit obligation (ABO)	165	190	292
Projected benefit obligation (PBO)	211	240	395
Entry age normal (EAN)	224	254	421
Projected value of benefits (PVB)	315	345	658
Annuitants only	260	310	376
Separated but not yet receiving benefits only	6	6	13

Source: Authors' calculations based on our model and inputs from seventy-seven Comprehensive Annual Financial Reports.

The lower panel of the left column decomposes the total into the member status as of 2009, where the categories are active participants, annuitants, and separated (no longer city-employed) participants not yet drawing benefits. Again, the liability due to current annuitants and separated workers is insensitive to the accrual method, since the accrual method is a question of how to treat future wage growth service by the employees who are currently in active employment. Around 45 percent of the PVB and around 60 percent of the ABO is due to individuals who already are retired.

The middle column of table 3-5 shows the results of discounting the cash flows using the AA+ municipal curve grossed up for a 25 percent tax preference. Focusing on the ABO, that raises the liability to $507 billion, which is 18 percent above the ABO at municipally chosen rates and only slightly above the liabilities on an as-stated basis (since the effect of the higher discount rate is mostly offset by the effect of the narrower accrual method). The PVB at the taxable muni rate is $662 billion, or 36 percent higher than the liabilities on an as-stated basis.

The right column of table 3-5 uses the procedure of discounting at Treasury rates, which we argued above is the preferred procedure for the ABO. Now the ABO is $681 billion. The PVB at Treasury rates is over $1 trillion, but that does not credit states at all for the ability to change the parameters on pensions owed to current employees. Of course, in states that Brown and Wilcox (2009) identifies as having strict constitutional guarantees (including Illinois, New York, and Louisiana), this method may in fact be the most appropriate reflection of the fact that some U.S. taxpayers will ultimately end up paying the expected benefits of all current employees.

Net of the assets in the plans, the unfunded liability is $383 billion using Treasury discounting, or over $5,300 per capita and over $185,000 per member. If on a per-member basis the unfunded liability is the same for the approximately 1 million local workers that are covered by municipal plans not in our sample, the total unfunded liability for all municipal plans in the United States is $574 billion.

Table 3-6 breaks down that calculation by sponsoring city or county and sorts the cities and counties in descending order of unfunded liability per household at Treasury rates.[9] Chicago is at the top of the list, with unfunded liabilities of $41,966 per city household, based on a per-person unfunded liability of $15,718. Note that represents the unfunded liability that would be owed even if all the Chicago plans were frozen today. New York City comes in second, with $38,886 per household; San Francisco third, with $34,940 per household; and Boston fourth, with $30,901 per household. In aggregate, each municipal household in the fifty cities and counties in our study owes $14,165 to current and retired employees of local pension systems.

Solvency Horizons for Local Systems

Here we examine the systems in the alternative way considered for states in Rauh (2010). We calculate how long the assets in the funds as of June 2009 could pay for benefits that were already promised as of 2009, assuming that targeted investment returns are in fact achieved. This method assumes that cities fully fund all future benefit accruals but do not make progress toward correcting the unfunded legacy liabilities. To the extent that the cities do make progress toward correcting the unfunded liability with large future contribution increases, they can potentially delay the day of reckoning. To the extent that the 8 percent returns

9. To calculate these figures, we collect 2009 population figures from the U.S. Census Bureau table "Annual Estimates of the Resident Population for Incorporated Places over 100,000" for cities and "Resident Population Estimates for the 100 Largest U.S. Counties." We then assume 2.67 people per household, consistent with the 2000 census data on household composition.

Table 3-6. *Municipal Liabilities in Descending Order of Unfunded Liability per Capita*[a]

Local government (number of plans)	Liabilities, stated basis, June 2009 (billions of dollars)	Liabilities (ABO), Treasury rate	Net pension assets (billions of dollars)	Unfunded liability (billions of dollars)	Unfunded liability/revenue (percent)	Unfunded liability per household (dollars)
Chicago (7[b])	46.3	66.6	21.8	44.8	763	41,966
New York City (5)	155.8	214.8	92.6	122.2	276	38,886
San Francisco (1)	16.3	22.6	11.9	8.7	306	34,940
Boston (1)	7.4	11.0	3.6	7.5	430	30,901
Detroit (2)	8.1	11.0	4.6	6.4	402	18,643
Los Angeles (3)	34.6	49.3	23.2	26.1	378	18,193
Philadelphia (1)	9.0	13.0	3.4	9.7	290	16,690
Cincinnati (1)	2.2	3.2	1.2	2.0	321	15,681
Baltimore (2)	4.4	6.4	2.7	3.7	260	15,420
Milwaukee (1)	4.4	6.7	3.3	3.4	687	14,853
Fairfax County (4)	8.3	11.1	5.5	5.6	169	14,415
Hartford (1)	1.2	1.6	0.9	0.7	249	14,333
St. Paul (1[c])	1.5	2.2	0.8	1.4	464	13,686
Jacksonville (2)	4.1	6.0	2.0	4.0	278	12,994
Dallas (2)	7.4	10.8	4.6	6.3	298	12,856
Contra Costa County (1)	6.3	8.7	3.7	5.0	425	12,771
Santa Barbara County (1)	2.3	3.3	1.4	1.8	329	11,995
Kern County (1)	4.2	5.6	2.0	3.6	612	11,919
San Jose (2)	5.4	7.5	3.4	4.1	321	11,391
Houston (3)	11.1	16.4	7.2	9.1	356	10,804

(continued)

Table 3-6. *Municipal Liabilities in Descending Order of Unfunded Liability per Capita*[a] (continued)

Local government (number of plans)	Liabilities, stated basis, June 2009 (billions of dollars)	Liabilities (ABO), Treasury rate	Net pension assets (billions of dollars)	Unfunded liability (billions of dollars)	Unfunded liability/revenue (percent)	Unfunded liability per household (dollars)
Nashville/Davidson County (1)	2.9	4.1	1.8	2.3	151	10,048
Arlington County (1)	1.5	2.0	1.2	0.8	103	10,000
Miami (2)	2.3	3.3	1.7	1.6	318	9,689
San Mateo County (1)	3.0	4.1	1.6	2.5	413	9,415
Seattle (1)	2.6	3.6	1.5	2.1	165	9,125
San Joaquin County (1)	2.7	3.8	1.5	2.3	525	9,119
Tacoma (1)	1.1	1.4	0.8	0.7	198	9,082
Sacramento County (1)	6.7	8.9	4.4	4.5	452	8,582
Memphis (2)	3.5	4.6	2.5	2.1	291	8,432
Fresno County (1)	3.6	5.1	2.3	2.9	843	8,401
Sonoma County (1)	2.0	2.6	1.1	1.5	397	8,394
Orange County (1)	11.5	15.6	6.2	9.3	604	8,233
Ventura County (1)	3.5	4.9	2.4	2.5	352	8,195
Montgomery County (1)	3.5	5.1	2.1	3.0	91	8,118
Alameda County (1)	5.7	8.0	3.8	4.2	353	7,579
Los Angeles County (1)	44.5	60.0	32.4	27.6	367	7,473
Fort Worth (1)	2.3	3.3	1.4	2.0	300	7,212
Anne Arundel County (1)	1.7	2.4	1.0	1.4	111	7,081
San Bernardino County (1)	7.0	9.6	4.5	5.1	407	6,716

Stanislaus County (1)	1.6	2.4	1.1	1.3	486	6,698
Baltimore County (1)	2.6	3.5	1.6	1.9	113	6,577
San Diego County (1)	9.2	13.4	6.2	7.2	631	6,329
DeKalb County (1)	1.8	2.3	1.0	1.4	186	4,873
Cook County (2)	10.9	14.3	6.1	8.2	365	4,112
Tulare County (1)	1.0	1.4	0.8	0.7	392	4,068
Fresno City (2)	1.6	2.4	1.7	0.7	172	3,647
Fulton County (1)	1.5	2.1	0.9	1.3	142	3,276
San Antonio (1)	2.4	3.4	1.8	1.7	140	3,201
Phoenix (1)	2.5	3.3	1.4	1.9	111	3,176
Tampa (2)	1.3	2.0	1.7	0.3	57	2,309
Total (78)	488.3	681.0	298.3	382.7		
Value-weighted					320	14,165
Equal-weighted					337	11,421

Source: Authors' calculations based on our model and inputs from seventy-seven Comprehensive Annual Financial Reports.

a. The first column shows liabilities on a stated basis as aggregated from government reports. The second column shows our calculation of accumulated liabilities discounted using the Treasury yield curve as of June 2009. The third column shows net pension assets. The fourth column shows the unfunded liability in dollar terms as of June 2009. The fifth shows the June 2009 unfunded liability as a share of 2006 revenue, where 2006 is the latest year for which detailed city and county revenues were available from the U.S. Census of Governments Tables on State and Local Government Finances (U.S. Census Bureau 2006). To calculate per household figures, we collect 2009 population figures from the U.S. Census Bureau table "Annual Estimates of the Resident Population for Incorporated Places over 100,000" (U.S. Census Bureau 2009a) for cities and "Resident Population Estimates for the 100 Largest U.S. Counties" (U.S. Census Bureau 2009b). We then assume 2.67 (two and two-thirds) people per household, consistent with the 2000 census data on household composition.

b. Included in the seven Chicago plans are three plans that are legally sponsored by districts related to Chicago and not fully by the city itself: the Chicago Teachers' Fund, the Metropolitan Water Reclamation District Retirement Fund of Greater Chicago, and the Retirement Plan for Chicago Transit Authority Employees.

c. The plan is the St. Paul Teachers' Association Retirement Fund, sponsored by a school district that is coterminous with the city of St. Paul and that receives funding from a variety of local and state sources.

that governments are hoping for are not achieved, the horizons on which existing assets are sufficient to pay already promised benefits are even shorter.

Various risk factors affect actual run-out dates. Run-outs can happen sooner if workers start retiring early in anticipation of problems, if taxpayers start moving out of troubled states, or if contributions are deferred or not made. Run-outs can happen later if states make fundamental reforms or borrow enough to fill the hole. Run-outs also will happen later if states use future contributions not to fund new benefits but to pay for the benefits of existing workers, although in that scenario run-outs are more likely to happen at some point because states are digging themselves into a deeper and deeper hole.

The first column of table 3-7 takes a reduced-form approach and simply takes the ratio of 2009 benefits to 2009 assets. For example, the top line shows that for Philadelphia this ratio is 5. If neither benefits nor assets grew at all, Philadelphia could pay that level of benefits for five years out of existing assets. Boston and Chicago could pay for eight years. At the other end of the spectrum, Fresno City could pay for twenty-three years.

Of course, benefit cash flows will grow, as shown in figure 3-1, even for the ABO.[10] Assets also are likely to grow through investment returns. The second column of the table assumes that assets earn 8 percent returns and that the assets currently under management plus the annual returns are used to pay benefits that have already been promised under the 2009 ABO. The year listed in column 2 is the year in which the assets will no longer be sufficient to pay the benefits under those assumptions. In Philadelphia, the assets would run out in 2015; in Boston and Chicago, they would run out in 2019.

The remaining columns show that if at that point the municipalities tried to switch to a pay-as-you-go system of paying the promised benefits, substantial shares of revenue would be consumed by benefits. Expected benefits are 25 percent of 2006 city revenues for Philadelphia in 2015; 40 percent of 2006 city revenues for Boston in 2019; and 78 percent of 2006 city revenues for Chicago in 2019. Assuming that city revenues grow at 3 percent a year, expected benefits are 19 percent of projected 2015 city revenues for Philadelphia; 27 percent of projected 2019 city revenues for Boston; and 53 percent of projected 2019 city revenues for Chicago.

Somewhat surprisingly, San Francisco, the city with the third-largest unfunded liability per household, avoids running out of funds until 2032. Its plan members

10. That is, even if promises were frozen at today's levels of service and salary, benefits would still grow because increasing numbers of people are retiring with increasingly generous benefits relative to the numbers and benefits of retirees who are dying.

Table 3-7. *Years That Existing Assets Are Adequate to Pay Accrued Benefits*[a]

			Expected benefits in year following		
Local government	*2009 ratio of benefits to assets*	*Year through which assets earning 8 percent pay ABO cash flows*	*Millions of dollars*	*Percent of 2006 revenue*	*Percent of projected revenue (revenue growth = 3 percent)*
Philadelphia (1)	5	2015	827.2	25	19
Boston (1)	8	2019	695.1	40	27
Chicago (7[b])	8	2019	4,551.1	78	53
Cincinnati (1)	9	2020	218.9	36	24
Jacksonville (2)	9	2020	437.8	31	20
St. Paul (1[c])	8	2020	151.3	49	32
New York City (5)	9	2021	15,976.2	36	23
Baltimore (2)	9	2022	480.1	34	21
DeKalb County (1)	12	2022	215.1	29	18
Fulton County (1)	10	2022	169.1	19	12
Kern County (1)	12	2022	480.4	82	51
Baltimore County (1)	11	2023	308.7	18	11
Detroit (2)	10	2023	872.7	55	33
Fort Worth (1)	12	2023	289.7	44	27
Phoenix (1)	11	2023	305.5	18	11
Sonoma County (1)	12	2023	242.0	65	39
Nashville/Davidson County (1)	11	2024	318.5	21	12
San Joaquin County (1)	14	2024	340.6	78	46
San Mateo County (1)	14	2024	360.7	59	35

(continued)

Table 3-7. *Years That Existing Assets Are Adequate to Pay Accrued Benefits*[a] (continued)

Local government	2009 ratio of benefits to assets	Year through which assets earning 8 percent pay ABO cash flows	Expected benefits in year following		
			Millions of dollars	Percent of 2006 revenue	Percent of projected revenue (revenue growth = 3 percent)
Seattle (1)	12	2024	310.6	24	14
Contra Costa County (1)	14	2025	795.1	68	39
Cook County (2)	14	2025	1,326.7	59	34
Montgomery County (1)	13	2025	441.8	14	8
Orange County (1)	15	2025	1,508.8	98	56
Anne Arundel County (1)	14	2026	229.8	19	10
Dallas (2)	14	2026	1,048.5	50	28
Fresno County (1)	14	2026	484.1	142	78
Houston (3)	16	2027	1,726.2	67	36
Los Angeles (3)	14	2027	4,586.5	66	36
Miami (2)	12	2027	251.4	51	27
San Jose (2)	16	2027	777.4	61	33
Santa Barbara County (1)	16	2027	330.2	59	32
Alameda County (1)	15	2028	824.4	69	36
Hartford (1)	11	2028	126.2	47	25
Memphis (2)	12	2028	390.9	53	28
Milwaukee (1)	13	2028	612.2	125	65

San Diego County (1)	15	2028	1,362.2	119	62
Stanislaus County (1)	15	2028	236.2	90	47
Fairfax County (4)	14	2029	1,076.0	32	16
San Bernardino County(1)	17	2029	1,116.1	90	45
Ventura County (1)	16	2029	531.2	76	38
Sacramento County (1)	19	2030	1,099.7	110	54
Tacoma (1)	16	2031	159.8	47	22
San Francisco City and County(1)	16	2032	2,595.1	74	34
Los Angeles County (1)	16	2033	6,844.8	91	41
San Antonio (1)	19	2033	431.7	37	16
Tulare County (1)	17	2034	157.0	93	41
Arlington County (1)	17	2038	254.5	32	12
Fresno City (2)	23	Never			
Tampa (2)	14	Never			

Source: Authors' calculations based on our model and inputs from seventy-seven Comprehensive Annual Financial Reports.

a. To be included, a system must pay out more than 20 percent of 2006 revenues at depletion year. The table shows the number of years that existing assets are adequate to pay for already promised benefits. The first column is a simple ratio of benefits to assets. The second column uses ABO cash flows and considers how long the existing assets in the funds can pay for benefits assuming the investment returns are 8 percent.

b. Included in the seven Chicago plans are three plans that are legally sponsored by districts related to Chicago and not fully by the city itself: the Chicago Teachers Fund, the Metropolitan Water Reclamation District Retirement Fund of Greater Chicago, and the Retirement Plan for Chicago Transit Authority Employees.

c. The plan is the St. Paul Teachers' Association Retirement Fund, sponsored by a school district that is coterminous with the city of St. Paul and that receives funding from a variety of local and state sources.

are relatively young, and its liability is disproportionally due to its current work force, not to retirees. Consequently its current pension payouts are low, at least relative to its total liability, and that pushes the run-out farther into the future. In addition, despite San Francisco's extremely large unfunded pension liability, its plan is *relatively* well funded. Only the two municipalities at the bottom of the run-out list, Fresno City and Miami, report higher funding levels than San Francisco.

These measures are meant to convey a sense of the adequacy of existing assets to pay for already promised benefits. Some cities may have plans in place under which future contributions will make up for unfunded legacy liabilities, but such plans often are abandoned in the face of a fiscal squeeze. For example, at the state level, Illinois and New Jersey have contribution requirements that at some point they promised that they would meet. But Illinois is now paying them with borrowed money, and New Jersey is paying only a small fraction of the "required" amount. The city of Chicago has actually received a funding break in the context of a recent reform that affected new workers in Illinois state plans, so that Chicago does not have to contribute $1.2 billion to the fund that it would have had to contribute otherwise (Chicago Tribune 2010). To the extent that cities create and adhere to plans to set aside money to pay for unfunded liabilities, the depletion of the funds can be delayed.

Conclusion

When measured using Treasury yields, the unfunded liabilities of municipal (city and county) pension plans in our sample add $574 billion to the $3 trillion in unfunded state-sponsored plans that we have documented in previous work. On average, each household in the cities and counties involved owes $14,165 in the form of off-balance-sheet debt to current and former municipal public employees, under the narrowest accounting measures, calculated strictly on the basis of work already performed and current levels of public employee wages and salaries. Under broader measures the debt is even greater.

Each of these households already owes almost $27,000 for its share of the $3 trillion state pension debt. The $14,165 of local debt raises the burden for each household in our sample by over 50 percent. If each metropolitan household were responsible for an equal share of the aggregate city and state unfunded liability, then each household in these areas would owe over $41,000.

These average statistics mask the fact that some cities and states are considerably worse off than others. For example, each household in Chicago owes $42,000 for the Chicago plans plus an additional $29,000 for its share of the Illinois state plans, for a total of $71,000 per household, or around $76 billion. It seems infeasible that Chicago, a city with approximately $0.3 billion in annual sales tax revenue and $0.8 billion in annual property tax revenue, can come up with payments for legacy liabilities of that magnitude. It seems more likely that the state of Illinois will end up bailing out Chicago, in which case all Illinois households will end up owing around $42,000. If that would in turn bankrupt Illinois, then the federal government might have to backstop the Illinois liabilities. The distribution of the unfunded liability across different types of taxpayers is an unresolved matter.

Part of the uncertainty stems from the fact that residents of one metropolitan area can move to another area in response to tax increases or spending cuts. At the metropolitan level the situation is especially stark, as residents can move to suburban areas in response to increased taxes and service cuts in urban areas. The fact that such a large burden of public employee pensions is concentrated in urban metropolitan areas threatens the long-run economic viability of those areas.

County tax systems and state allocation formulas may play a role in reallocating resources, which might limit the ability of households to flee to nearby suburbs. However, the economic incentives are especially strong when a city borders on other cities, or even other states, that are in better financial health. For example, New Hampshire is just over thirty miles from downtown Boston; Delaware is only around twenty miles from downtown Philadelphia; Indiana is less than twenty miles from downtown Chicago; and Kentucky is only five miles from downtown Cincinnati.

What is clear is that state and local governments in the United States have massive public pension liabilities on their hands and that they are not far from the point where those liabilities will impact their ability to operate. Given the legal protections that many states accord to liabilities, which in a number of cases derive from state constitutions, attempts to limit liabilities with benefit cuts for existing workers will go only so far (Brown and Wilcox 2009; Novy-Marx and Rauh 2010b). The question going forward is how the burden will be distributed between urban and non-urban areas, between state and local governments, among the more and less fiscally responsible states, and between local governments and the federal government. If that question remains unresolved, state and local fiscal crises may translate into losses for municipal bondholders.

References

Barro, Robert. 1976. "Rational Expectations and the Role of Monetary Policy." *Journal of Monetary Economics* 2, no. 1, pp. 1–32.
Brown, Jeffrey, and David Wilcox. 2009. "Discounting State and Local Pension Liabilities." *American Economic Review* 99, no. 2, pp. 538–42.

Bulow, Jeremy. 1982. "What Are Corporate Pension Liabilities?" *Quarterly Journal of Economics* 97, no. 3, pp. 435–52.

Chicago Tribune. 2010. "Chicago's $20 Billion Pension Problem." November 17, 2010.

Duffie, Darrell, and Kenneth J. Singleton. 1997. "An Econometric Model of the Term Structure of Interest-Rate Swap Yields." *Journal of Finance* 52, no. 4, pp. 1287–1321.

Fisher, Stanley. 1975. "The Demand for Index Bonds." *Journal of Political Economy* 83, no. 3, pp. 509–34.

Krishnamurthy, Arvind, and Annette Vissing-Jorgensen. 2008. "The Aggregate Demand for Treasury Debt." Kellogg School of Management Working Paper.

Lintner, L. 1965. "The Valuation of Risk Assets and the Selection of Risky Investments in Stock Portfolios and Capital Budgets." *Review of Economic Statistics* 47, no. 1, pp. 13–37.

Longstaff, Francis A. 2004. "The Flight-to-Liquidity Premium in U.S. Treasury Bond Prices." *Journal of Business* 77, no. 3, pp. 511–26.

Modigliani, Franco, and Merton H. Miller. 1958. "The Cost of Capital, Corporation Finance, and the Theory of Investment." *American Economic Review* 48, no. 3, pp. 261–97.

Novy-Marx, Robert, and Joshua D. Rauh. 2009. "The Risks and Liabilities of State-Sponsored Pension Plans." *Journal of Economic Perspectives* 23, no. 4, pp. 191–210.

———. 2010a. "Public Pension Promises: How Big Are They and What Are They Worth?" *Journal of Finance,* forthcoming (http://papers.ssrn.com/sol3/papers.cfm?abstract_id=1352608).

———. 2010b. "Policy Options for State Pension Systems and Their Impact on Plan Liabilities." *Journal of Pension Economics and Finance,* forthcoming.

Poterba, James, and Arturo Ramirez Verdugo. 2008. "Portfolio Substitution and the Revenue Cost of Exempting State and Local Government Interest Payments from Federal Income Tax." Working Paper 14439 (Cambridge, Mass.: Bureau of Economic Research).

Rauh, Joshua. 2010. "Are State Public Pensions Sustainable? Why the Federal Government Should Worry about State Pension Liabilities," *National Tax Journal* 63, no. 3, pp. 585–601.

Sharpe, W. F. 1964. "Capital Asset Prices: A Theory of Market Equilibrium under Conditions of Risk." *Journal of Finance* 19, no. 3, pp. 425–42.

Society of Actuaries. 2000. "The RP-2000 Mortality Tables" (www.soa.org/files/pdf/rp00_mortalitytables.pdf).

Treynor, Jack L. 1961. "Toward a Theory of the Market Value of Risky Assets." Unpublished paper.

U.S. Census Bureau. 2006. "Tables on State and Local Government Finance" (www.census.gov/govs/estimate/historical_data_2006.html).

———. 2008. "State and Local Government Retirement Systems" (www2.census.gov/govs/retire/2008ret05a.xls).

———. 2009a. "Annual Estimates of the Resident Population for Incorporated Places over 100,000" (www.census.gov/popest/cities/tables/SUB-EST2009-01.xls).

———. 2009b. "Resident Population Estimates for the 100 Largest U.S. Counties" (www.census.gov/popest/counties/tables/CO-EST2009-07.xls).

Woodford, Michael. 1990. "Public Debt as Private Liquidity." *American Economic Review* 80, no. 2, pp. 382–88.

OLIVIA S. MITCHELL

4

Managing Risks in Defined Contribution Plans: What Does the Future Hold?

I N MANY COUNTRIES, traditional defined benefit (DB) pensions have become less popular over the last two decades, during which they have been supplemented—and in some cases replaced—by defined contribution (DC) plans. While DC plans have many appealing features, including transparency and portability, they also require participants to take an active role in managing them to achieve their ultimate purpose, namely, meeting participants' consumption needs in retirement. And, noting that participants sometimes have difficulty managing their retirement plans effectively, some critics have charged that DC plans are not up to the task. Accordingly, analysts and policymakers are now asking whether DC plans should be completely overhauled in order to better meet national retirement objectives. This chapter addresses these issues by evaluating the main retirement risks confronting participants in and sponsors of DC plans and by discussing how markets and regulators are responding to those risks.[1] The chapter concludes with a brief mention of key lessons and policy implications for the future of DC plan risk management.

This topic is of interest since pension assets represent millions of workers' retirement hopes; they also represent a key source of global financial capital. In

The author acknowledges support from the Pension Research Council and Boettner Center at the Wharton School of the University of Pennsylvania.
1. This discussion draws on Mitchell (2010a, b).

Figure 4-1. *Pension Assets of Selected Countries as a Percentage of Total Global Pension Assets*[a]

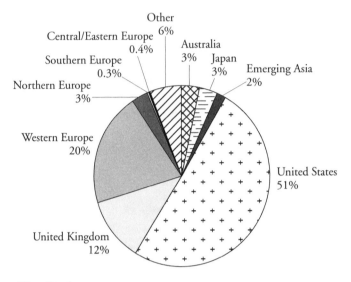

Source: Allianz (2010).
a. Numbers have been rounded.

2009, worldwide retirement funds amounted to an estimated US$24 trillion, projected to grow to more than $34 trillion in 2014 (Allianz 2010); see figure 4-1. Pension assets represent a substantial portion of the world's wealth, equivalent to two-thirds of GDP on average for the nations depicted in figure 4-2 and more than total national output in some cases. The United States has the largest retirement asset pool, $16.5 trillion in 2010, of which $4.2 trillion was held in employer-based defined contribution (DC) retirement plans (ICI 2010). Nevertheless, pensions have not been immune to market shocks, suffering mightily with the recent sharp drop in equity markets (see figure 4-3). In 2008 in the United States, for instance, pension assets fell by more than 20 percent, coinciding unfortunately with the moment when the aging baby boomers began to claim benefits (Moore 2010; Allianz 2010). Figure 4-4 shows that rates of return on pension fund assets were sharply negative in 2008 across a broad swath of OECD countries, a shock from which plan sponsors and participants are still recovering.

It is sometimes argued that market shocks have a more potent influence on retirement preparedness for those in DC plans than for those in DB plans.[2]

2. See Burtless (2008); for a related discussion see Bosworth and Burtless (2010).

Figure 4-2. *Pension Assets as a Percentage of GDP in Selected OECD Countries, 2009*

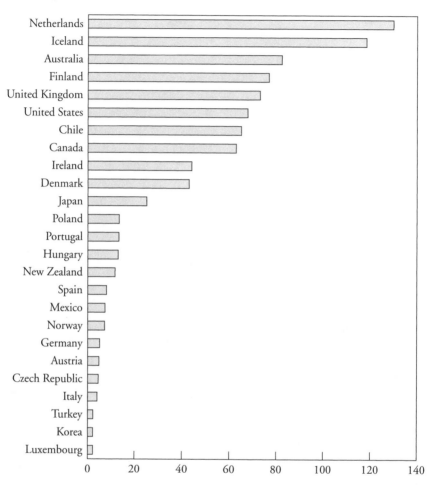

Source: Derived from OECD (2010).

That is because in the former investment drops are immediately recorded in workers' and pensioners' accounts, whereas in a DB plan, a drop in asset values requires sponsors (and sometimes active workers) to make remedial contributions to fill the gap. Yet DB promises often cannot be met if sponsors close down their businesses with insufficient assets to cover pension promises. As table 4-1 illustrates, with the notable exception of retirement assets in Japan and Canada,

Figure 4-3. *U.S., European Monetary Union (EMU), and Emerging Markets Equity Market Price Indexes, 1985–2010*

Percent

Source: Author's computations from Thompson Reuters Datastream (http://online.thomsonreuters. com/datastream/).

at least one-third and sometimes the bulk of retirement assets in many large economies are now held in defined contribution plans: some 43 percent, or close to $10 trillion, is managed in DC plan structures today. Further, industry projections estimate that DC assets will rise faster than DB plan assets in the future, including in Japan where DC plans now cover 3.5 million participants (in 2009), up from only 88,000 participants in 2001 (Nomura 2009; Nishiyama and Nakanishi 2010). In other words, it seems clear that DC plans are here to stay and that DB plans will continue to decline in coverage. For that reason it is crucial to focus on the question of how best to manage the risks particular to DC pensions.

Identifying Risks and Solutions

It is useful to classify the key challenges facing the DC system into four types of risk: *individual* risk, *institutional* risk, *country* risk, and *global* risk. The following discussion first describes what is meant by each type of risk and then identifies some responses to each type.[3]

3. This risk classification was introduced by Mitchell (2010b).

Figure 4-4. *Pension Returns in Selected OECD Countries, 2008–09*

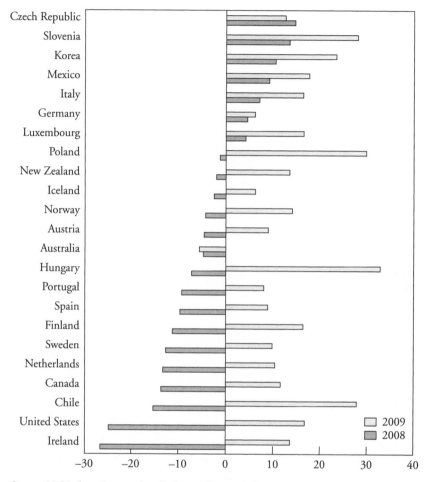

Source: OECD (http://stats.oecd.org/Index.aspx?DatasetCode=PNNI_NEW).

Risks Confronting Individuals and Their Families

The conventional economic view of the life-cycle problem is that consumers will save and invest during youth and middle age in order to have income and/or assets to live on after labor market earnings cease. Pensions can play a very central role in the accumulation phase and later in the payout process, in that they represent deferred earnings dedicated to retirement consumption. (Buying a home and paying down one's home mortgage was once seen in the same light,

Table 4-1. *Split between Defined Contribution and Defined Benefit Pension Plans in Selected Countries*

Country	Pension assets[a]	Percent	
		DC	*DB*
Total	23,290	59	41
United States[b]	13,196	55	45
Japan	3,152	1	99
United Kingdom[c]	1,791	39	61
Canada	1,213	3	97
Australia	996	82	18
Netherlands	990	8	92
Switzerland	583	58	42
Germany	411	35	65
Brazil	392	66	34
South Africa	201	73	27
France	178	25	75
Ireland	102	39	61
Hong Kong	85	78	22

Source: Towers Watson (2010).
a. Assets in billions of 2009 U.S. dollars.
b. Includes individual retirement accounts.
c. Excludes personal pensions and stakeholder pensions.

prior to the collapse of the housing bubble.) During the decumulation phase of life, the task is to draw down assets in an orderly manner, not too quickly, to avoid running out of money too soon.

In practice, of course, implementing the life-cycle model is fraught with problems. One is widespread financial illiteracy, combined with failure to devise and execute retirement saving plans. Because half the population will outlive its life expectancy, there is a substantial chance that some retirees will run out of money in old age. For instance, several recent surveys asked U.S. residents three financial literacy questions (Lusardi and Mitchell 2007a, b; Lusardi and Mitchell 2008; Lusardi, Mitchell, and Curto 2010):

—Percentage calculation: If the chance of getting a disease is 10 percent, how many people out of 1,000 would be expected to get the disease?

—Lottery division: If five people all have the winning number in the lottery and the prize is $2 million, how much will each of them get?

Table 4-2. *Financial Literacy among Early Baby Boomers*[a]

| | Percent | |
Question	Correct	Incorrect or don't know
Percentage calculation	83.5	16
Lottery division	55.9	43.1
Compound interest	17.8	81.7

Source: Adapted from Lusardi and Mitchell (2009).

a. Early baby boomer sample (N = 1,984) surveyed in the Health and Retirement Study weighted using household weights. Percentages may not sum to 100 due to missing data on a few respondents; values conditional on being asked the question.

—Compound interest: Let's say you have $200 in a savings account. The account earns 10 percent interest a year. How much would you have in the account at the end of two years?

Results for a nationally representative sample of older U.S. respondents appear in table 4-2. On one hand, almost 84 percent of the respondents—in their mid-fifties at the time—could correctly compute the percentage question. More troubling was the fact that only slightly over half of the boomers could accurately divide $2 million by 5. But most troubling was the fact that only 18 percent of this nationally representative sample of Americans in their fifties understands the principle of compound interest. Of those responding incorrectly, around two-fifths carried out a simple interest computation, whereas three-fifths either failed to answer at all or responded with a plainly incorrect answer. That is of concern because most people in their mid-fifties already have taken numerous financial actions, including taking out student loans, borrowing on credit cards, buying cars on time, and taking out home mortgages. Since this group does so poorly at both simple numeracy and financial concepts, it is little wonder that their retirement finances are not in order.

Research also shows that financial literacy is a strong predictor of planning for retirement and succeeding in accumulating retirement assets (Lusardi and Mitchell 2007a). Better-educated people do perform better, yet even so, only 18 percent of households on the verge of retirement are relatively successful at devising retirement plans and executing them (at least some of the time). Furthermore, those who succeed at retirement planning are almost three times as wealthy as those who do not. It is worth noting that these results are robust to tests for reverse causality (Lusardi, Mitchell, and Curto 2010; Behrman and others

2010)—that is, to tests of whether financial literacy drives planning and wealth or vice versa. These findings, along with those in Bernheim, Garrett, and Maki (2001), confirm that financial literacy has an important and independent impact, suggesting that strengthening consumer knowledge of basic economics and finance could enhance retirement well-being.

Employers who offer DC pensions can and often do play a role in helping combat employee illiteracy and inertia regarding retirement saving. For instance, some firms provide workers with retirement seminars, financial well-being calculators, and benefit estimators to enhance retirement planning and build pension savings (Clark and others 2006). Workplace pension policies such as automatic enrollment and commitment saving programs also have made substantial inroads, inducing workers to save more by enrolling them by default into DC pension plans.[4] Such default plans require the employer to select prefabricated investment portfolios such as life-cycle or target maturity date funds, in which the fund management gradually moves assets into less risky holdings as the worker ages. Evidence suggests that this approach can improve participant asset allocation patterns and enhance retirement accumulations over time, particularly for low-paid workers, women, and less financially literate participants (Mitchell and others 2009).

Another source of risk facing participants in DC plans stems from fluctuations in labor market earnings. Even in good economic times, people lose their jobs and experience periods without steady labor income, and human capital risk is widespread. Indeed the canonical smooth "hump-shaped" labor income profile so often assumed in economic modeling turns out to be relatively rare in practice (see figure 4-5). For instance, Mitchell and Turner (2010) cites evidence indicating that workers' actual lifetime pay profiles turn out to be quite erratic due to periods of zero and low earnings. Only 14 percent of U.S. workers fit the classic hump-shaped profile; the same fraction had *sagging* real earnings in the middle years, another group had lifetime *flat* earnings, and yet another group had *declining earnings from a fairly young age* (compare Bosworth, Burtless, and Steuerle 2000). Such patterns are critical in DC plans, in which contributions depend on pay and are made only when people are employed. Furthermore, the early years tend to matter most, because savings can earn compound interest over a longer period.

We turn next to the risk that retirees confront due to uncertainty over longevity. That becomes a key consideration for DC plan participants in countries such as the United States, since retirees there are not required to buy lifelong income at the point of retirement and most plan sponsors do not offer the option of an in-plan payout annuity. Instead, retirees may withdraw their entire pension accumulation

---

4. See, for instance, Thaler and Benartzi (2004).

Figure 4-5. *Patterns of Lifetime Earnings Excluding and Including Zero Earners*[a]

Panel A. Low-income workers with rising life-cycle earnings, with and without zero earners

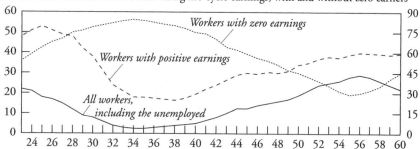

Panel B. Middle-income workers with rising life-cycle earnings, with and without zero earners

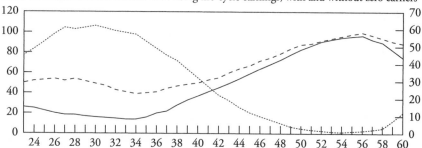

Panel C. High-income workers with rising life-cycle earnings, with and without zero earners

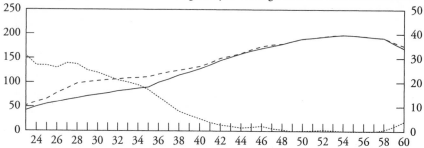

Source: Mitchell and Turner (2010), derived from Bosworth, Burtless, and Steuerle (2000).

a. Average earnings as a percentage of economy-wide average earnings on left scale; percentage of individuals with zero earnings in each year measured on right scale.

(with tax consequences), take the money out gradually in a phased withdrawal approach, or roll the money into a tax-qualified account and use that to purchase lifetime payout annuities. But in the United States (as in many other countries), few retirees purchase annuity payout products, reducing the longevity protection afforded to DB plan participants (Mitchell, Piggott, and Takayama 2011).

In theory, payout annuities constitute an essential tool for retirement planning, since most retirees would benefit when they exchange a premium payment for an insurer's commitment to pay an income benefit until death.[5] That is still true even when taking into account the adverse selection that arises when people who buy payout annuities live longer than average. Yet people tend to underannuitize, partly because they underestimate the chances of living to a very old age and hence subject themselves to the "tail risk" of living well beyond their life expectancy (Brown and others 1999; Brown, Mitchell, and Poterba 2000; Brown and others 2001; Brown, Mitchell, and Poterba 2002). Over time, that risk is exacerbated by cohort-wide mortality improvement, which imposes on retirees the additional uncertainty of evolving life tables (see Dowd, Blake, and Cairns 2007). Another factor retarding annuity market development is that confidence in the life insurance industry has been shaken in the wake of problems with impaired insurance company assets and other market shocks; in addition, some insurers have required government support due to depleted reserves.

In response to these important and often underestimated sources of retirement risk in DC plans, some critics contend that DC plans are simply not up to the job. For instance, Munnell and Sundén (2004) characterizes them as "coming up short," since some workers save too little, make uninformed investment decisions, and borrow the money rather than save it for old age. Nevertheless, such criticisms overlook the role of government Social Security benefits in crowding out low-wage workers' need to save for retirement; furthermore, "leakage" from tax-qualified accounts is relatively small (Brady 2008). It also is true that DC plans enable labor mobility and delayed retirement, whereas DB plans tend to penalize continued work past an early retirement age (Fields and Mitchell 1984). Interestingly, relatively few people appear to have responded to recent macroeconomic shocks by pushing back their retirement dates (Bosworth and Burtless 2010; Goda, Shoven, and Slavov 2010; Gustman, Steinmeier, and Tabatabai 2010; Coile and Levine 2006). That may be because few older workers currently are directly exposed to equity: only those older Americans in the top decile of the wealth distribution hold as much as 20 percent of their assets in stocks (see table 4-3), and equity-holding is

5. See Dus, Maurer, and Mitchell (2005); Horneff and others (2007, 2009, 2010); Maurer, Mitchell, and Rogalla (2010); and Mitchell, Poterba, and Warshawsky (1999).

Table 4-3. *Stock Market Exposure of Older U.S. Households, by Wealth Decile, in the Health and Retirement Study*[a]

Source of wealth	Average asset value for respondents in indicated total wealth percentile						
	1–10	*11–20*	*21–40*	*41–60*	*61–80*	*81–90*	*91–100*
Total wealth ($000)	51.7	135.3	587.4	1,086.2	1,807.8	1,421.4	2,573.9
Wealth held in stocks/ total wealth (%)	1.5	2.3	6.1	9.3	11.9	16	22.6

Source: Derived from Gustman, Steinmeier, and Tabatai (2010).

a. Households with top and bottom 1 percent of wealth are excluded. Wealth in stocks includes share of defined contribution accounts in stocks, share of IRA accounts in stocks, and direct stockholdings. Total wealth includes Social Security and pension wealth, IRA assets, and net housing wealth.

minuscule among those in the bottom half of the wealth distribution. Among DC account holders, there was a modest flight to safety during the financial turmoil of 2008–09 (Tang and Mitchell 2010; Vanguard 2010), but the amounts transferred were not substantial and trading apparently has not altered participants' anticipated portfolio performance.

Pension System Risks

Institutional risk—that is, the possibility that the retirement system itself might fail—is a second type of risk. The sad reality is that the financial crisis has brought into sharp focus the extraordinarily poor condition of pension systems all over the world, including the underfunding of U.S. corporate and public DB plans. Though corporate plans in the United States have the backing of a government reinsurance program, as do corporate plans in the United Kingdom, such government entities also often face financial problems of their own (Brown 2010).

In the DC world, the market downturn has led some to suggest that guarantees must be embedded in pension accounts so that workers are not too exposed to equity risk. While that proposal has some appeal, guarantees can be extremely costly, and the more generous the guarantee, the more expensive it becomes. Japan's 401(k)-type model requires that at least one fund be principal guaranteed; in that case, after forty years, the member is sure to get back at least the money that he or she put in (with a zero rate of return). While that type of guarantee is relatively inexpensive to provide, guaranteeing a bond return costs much more, from 16 percent to 20 percent or more of annual contributions (Lachance and Mitchell, 2003; Lachance, Mitchell, and Smetters 2003). Furthermore, if guarantees were to be offered in the DC context, it would be crucial to limit investors' portfolios so that people do not "game" the guarantee by investing only in extremely

Figure 4-6. *Mean and 95th Percentile of Remaining Health Care Costs, Including Nursing Home, by Age*

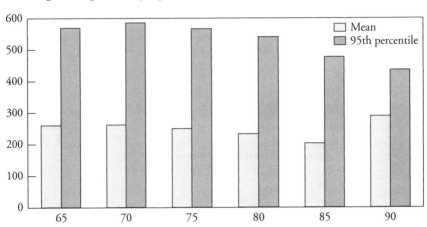

Source: Webb and Zhivan (2010).

risky assets. In other words, including guaranteed products in DC plan menus may be attractive but guarantees cannot be provided for free.

National Risk Exposure

National factors also influence retirement risk management. Unfortunately, national risks tend to be highly unpredictable; political risk, for example, means that future tax and transfer policy is usually rather uncertain. One need only recall Argentina's recent government takeover of national pension assets, justified at the time by the suggestion that retirees would be "safer" with government IOUs instead of volatile capital market assets. Another aspect of national risk has to do with the future of government old-age (Social Security) and retiree healthcare provision. In the United States at least, anticipated healthcare costs, including nursing home care, are highly uncertain, depending on the as-yet unknown evolution of efforts to control Medicare costs, which must be controlled if system finances are to balance. Moreover, even if expected average health costs are relatively predictable, such costs are very skewed in practice, implying that any given household might need half a million dollars or more to pay for old-age healthcare needs (Fronstin 2008); see figure 4-6.

The delicate state of many nations' old-age social security systems also is worth noting. In the United States, for instance, anticipated shortfalls exceed $15 trillion (in expected present value), a sum large enough to substantially challenge the

Figure 4-7. *Projected Social Security Tax Revenues and Outlays and System Shortfalls under Currently Scheduled Benefits*

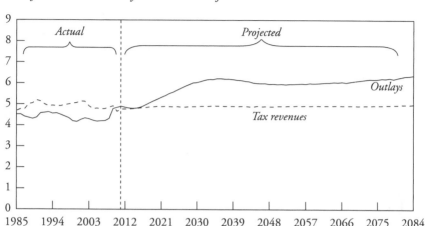

Source: CBO (2010).

system's long-term viability (see figure 4-7). That is because under existing law, future benefits will grow faster than prices and contribute to the system's projected cash flow shortfall. The 2001 President's Commission to Strengthen Social Security, a bipartisan group, proposed to rectify the problem by reducing the *growth rate of future benefits* while preserving benefits in current dollars (Cogan and Mitchell 2003). In that case, no benefit cuts would be required in real terms, compared to today's benefits, and the system would return to solvency.[6] Unfortunately, the commission's proposals were reported at a time when national attention had turned to other matters, and inaction—along with the recession and financial system bailouts—has exacerbated Medicare and Social Security shortfalls.

Global Risk Considerations

Last but certainly not least is global retirement risk. Probably relatively little to enhance retirement security and strengthen DC plans with respect to global risk is feasible in the near term. It does appear that observers need not have worried that baby boomers would drive down equity markets and housing values by retiring and redeeming their assets, since the global asset meltdown happened before most

6. Indeed, that would also allow some additional benefit enhancements for the lifetime low-wage workforce. In addition, the commission was asked by the president to design voluntary personal accounts in such a way that it left the system actuarially neutral; that is, it would not cost the system or benefit it.

boomers retired! The central problem with global risk management, of course, is that for the most part the risks cannot be diversified. In other words, for the purposes of risk pooling, diversifying one's portfolio with global investments seems less attractive today than in the past. Likewise, spreading risk across generations with pay-as-you-go social security systems also is dangerous in the face of global aging: if future generations are likely to be far smaller than previous ones, very few workers will be available to support the long-lived elderly (Shoven and Schieber 1999). An alternative approach might be to develop formal markets in which today's workers could "commit" to trade claims over consumption with those as yet unborn (Smetters 2004), but that is still only a theoretical possibility; there is no effective market for such claims at present.

Lessons and Implications for Defined Contribution Plan Risk Management

As DC plans have expanded and DB plans have declined around the world, many new ideas have emerged to enhance the resilience of the DC system. For instance, today many employers offering DC plans provide automatic enroll-ment, which is proven to increase substantially workers' propensity to save (Madrian and Shea 2001). Other new arrangements include commitment saving devices or techniques to foster desired changes in behavior, such as the Save More Tomorrow (Smart) plan devised in Thaler and Benartzi (2004).[7] Analysts also have demonstrated that pension asset allocation patterns can be swayed by surprising and even welfare-reducing factors (compare Mitchell and Utkus 2004). For instance, when employers make contributions in company stock—as occurred most notoriously in the case of Enron, which then went bankrupt—employees are more likely to invest their own contributions in the same undiversified stock. Conversely, if a plan sponsor defaults workers into so-called life-cycle or target maturity date funds, evidence shows that the employees remain in the funds for the long term; as a result, younger workers tend to end up with professionally managed blended funds holding more equity and older workers tend to hold more fixed income. As Tang and others (2010) shows, that is likely to enhance workers' asset allocation choices and expected performance.

One area in which much remains to be done is management of DC assets at and into retirement. Currently in the United States, around three-quarters of DC assets are paid out as lump-sum cash-outs instead of income annuities (McGill and others 2004), a potentially problematic result if retirees end up outliving their

---

7. For other related ideas, see Choi and others (2002).

resources. That tendency could be countered if employers offer annuities rather than lump-sum payouts as the default option at retirement. Singapore has gone a step further, requiring that older workers purchase deferred annuities to protect them against longevity risk (Fong, Mitchell, and Koh 2010). Nevertheless, when the U.S. Department of Labor recently sought comments on including annuities as defaults for 401(k) plans, numerous objections were lodged, making it clear that implementing a mandate here is unlikely in the short term (Ebeling 2010).

In the larger sphere, of course, pension plans and those that they cover must also confront other key challenges associated with political, demographic, and financial uncertainty in the near term. Political risk in the United States is salient, due to the fact that U.S. tax law is in flux—in fact, for the last several years, Congress has repeatedly debated how to overhaul the income and estate tax system. Similarly, politicians thus far have not dealt with the looming insolvency in Social Security and Medicare, implying that workers and retirees cannot readily project what they can expect from those sources and hence how much they should save and withdraw from their pension assets. Demographic trends also are uncertain: declining fertility seems to be a given in most developed countries, along with probably longer lifespans, though increases in morbidity due to obesity could cut in the opposite direction. And if the future continues to be characterized by continued low returns and equity market volatility, that would likely make it much harder to build up retirement assets and finance a long retirement period.

Financial markets may help in responding to these problems with a new range of innovative products that would allocate risk more efficiently across stakeholders (Mitchell and others 2006). For example, products for an aging population could include reverse mortgages, inflation-protected payout annuities, better long-term care insurance, survivor and mortality bonds, and mortality securitization. Nevertheless, those products have been slow to find a market due to uncertainty regarding future mortality trends and information asymmetry in the markets. Those shortcomings may prompt public sector entities to find ways to partner with the private sector in order to develop better databases to facilitate better risk management for an aging world (Mitchell and others 2006).

Conclusions

Retirement security requires that workers have access to successful, reliable, and resilient mechanisms that enable them to save while young and transfer that wealth to a future time when they need to draw the assets down in the form of reliable and predictable old-age income streams. But all too often in the past, retirement saving arrangements have proven risky and difficult to maintain, particularly because some of the key players—employers, financial institutions, and governments—have failed to deliver on the promises that they made.

Indeed, many public and private defined benefit pensions are in serious trouble today, having fallen prey to underfunding, to asset/liability mismatching, and sometimes to strategic manipulation for purposes other than those intended. By contrast, defined contribution pensions have firmly established themselves as the mainstay of retirement provision in Australia, Chile, and Singapore, and they are growing in much of the rest of the world. DC plans have many positive features: they can offer an attractive framework for building a secure retirement while allowing the necessary labor mobility that a modern marketplace requires; they provide an opportunity for workers to tailor their own portfolios to their risk tolerance by using diverse investment menus; and they allow people to pass on unspent assets to future generations. And from the perspective of an employer, DC plans are attractive in that they relieve management of the need to continue paying people benefits long after they have departed the active workforce, shifting both funding and longevity risk to the retiree. DC plans are helping millions of workers invest their money and accumulate retirement assets.

There are nevertheless tasks remaining to ensure retirement security in the new financial environment. Many DC participants still save too little, fail to diversify and invest too much in their own company stock, and suffer from "lump-sum illusion"—believing that a relatively small nest egg will be sufficient to live on during their golden years. As a result, they may fail to annuitize at retirement, taking a chance instead that they will die before the money runs out. These remaining shortcomings in the DC model can be rectified, building on greater understanding of the role of behavior in household financial decisionmaking.

References

Allianz. 2010. "Big and Getting Bigger: Despite Financial Crisis Global Retirement Market Expected to Grow to 36 Trillion until 2020" (https://www.allianz.com/static-resources/en/press/media/documents/demographic_pulse/dempulse_310_engl_final.pdf).

Behrman, Jere, and others. 2010. "Financial Literacy, Schooling, and Wealth Accumulation." NBER Working Paper 16542. Cambridge, Mass.: National Bureau of Economic Research.

Bernheim, Douglas, Daniel M. Garrett, and Dean Maki. 2001. "Education and Saving: The Long-Term Effects of High School Financial Curriculum Mandates." *Journal of Public Economics* 80, no. 3 (June), pp. 435–65.

Bosworth, Barry, and Gary Burtless. 2010. "Recessions, Wealth Destruction, and the Timing of Retirement." 12th Annual Joint Conference of the Retirement Research Consortium, Washington, August 5–6.

Bosworth, Barry, Gary Burtless, and C. Eugene Steuerle. 2000. "Lifetime Earnings Patterns, the Distribution of Future Social Security Benefits, and the Impact of Pension Reform." *Social Security Bulletin* 63, no. 4, pp. 74–98.

Brady, Peter. 2008. "Can 401(k) Plans Provide Adequate Retirement Resources?" Washington: Investment Company Institute (December).

Brown, Jeffrey R. 2010. *Private Markets and Public Insurance Programs.* Washington: American Enterprise Institute Press.

Brown, Jeffrey, Olivia S. Mitchell, and James Poterba. 2002. "Mortality Risk, Inflation Risk, and Annuity Products." In *Innovations in Financing Retirement,* edited by Zvi Bodie, Brett Hammond, and Olivia S. Mitchell, pp. 175–97. University of Pennsylvania Press.

———. 2000. "The Role of Real Annuities and Indexed Bonds in an Individual Accounts Retirement Program." In *Risk Aspects of Investment-Based Social Security Reform,* edited by John Campbell and Martin Feldstein, pp. 321–60. University of Chicago Press.

Brown, Jeffrey, and others. 1999. "Taxing Retirement Income: Nonqualified Annuities and Distributions from Qualified Accounts." *National Tax Journal* 52, no. 3 (September), pp. 563–92.

Brown, Jeffrey, and others. 2001. *The Role of Annuity Markets in Financing Retirement.* MIT Press.

Burtless, Gary. 2008. "Stock Market Fluctuations and Retiree Incomes: An Update." Brookings Institution (www.brookings.edu/papers/2008/1031_market_burtless.aspx).

Choi, James, and others. 2002. "Defined Contribution Pensions: Plan Rules, Participant Decisions, and the Path of Least Resistance." In *Tax Policy and the Economy,* vol. 16, edited by James M. Poterba, pp. 67–113. MIT Press.

Clark, Robert, and others. 2006. "Retirement Plans and Saving Decisions: The Role of Information and Education." *Journal of Pension Economics and Finance* (March), pp. 45–67.

Cogan, John F., and Olivia S. Mitchell. 2003. "Perspectives from the President's Commission on Social Security Reform." *Journal of Economic Perspectives* 17, no. 2 (Spring).

Coile, Courtney, and Philip Levine. 2006. "Bulls, Bears, and Retirement Behavior." *Industrial and Labor Relations Review* 59, no. 3 (April), pp. 408–29.

Congressional Budget Office (CBO). 2010. *CBO's 2010 Long-Term Projections for Social Security: Additional Information* (www.cbo.gov/ftpdocs/119xx/doc11943/10-22-SocialSecurity_chartbook.pdf).

Dowd, Kevin, David Blake, and Andrew J. G. Cairns. 2007. "The Myth of Methuselah and the Uncertainty of Death: The Mortality Fan Charts." Pensions Institute Working Paper (November).

Dus, Ivica, Raimond Maurer, and Olivia S. Mitchell. 2005. "Betting on Death and Capital Markets in Retirement: A Shortfall Risk Analysis of Life Annuities versus Phased Withdrawal Plans." *Financial Services Review* 14, pp. 169–96.

Ebeling, Ashlea. 2010. "Anti-Annuity Sentiment Boils Over before DOL Hearings." *Forbes,* September 14.

Fields, Gary S., and Olivia S. Mitchell. 1984. *Retirement, Pensions, and Social Security.* MIT Press.

Fong, Joelle H. Y., Olivia S. Mitchell, and Benedict S. K. Koh. 2010. "Longevity Risk Management in Singapore's National Pension System." *Journal of Risk and Insurance* (December), pp. 1–21.

Fronstin, Paul. 2008. *Savings Needed to Fund Health Insurance and Health Care Expenses in Retirement.* EBRI Issue Brief 295. Washington: Employee Benefit Research Institute.

Goda, Gopi Shah, John Shoven, and Sita Nataraj Slavov. 2010. "Does Stock Market Performance Influence Retirement Expectations?" Paper presented at the 12th Annual Conference of the Retirement Research Consortium, Washington, August 5–6.

Gustman, Alan, Thomas L. Steinmeier, and Nahid Tabatabai. 2010. "What the Stock Market Decline Means for the Financial Security and Retirement Choices of the Near-Retirement Population." *Journal of Economic Perspectives* 24, no. 1 (Winter), pp. 161–82.

Horneff, Wolfram, and others. 2007. "Following the Rules: Integrating Asset Allocation and Annuitization in Retirement Portfolios." *Insurance: Mathematics and Economics* 42, pp. 396–408.

———. 2009. "Asset Allocation and Location over the Life Cycle with Survival-Contingent Payouts." *Journal of Banking and Finance* 33, no. 9 (September), pp. 1688–99.

———. 2010. "Variable Payout Annuities and Dynamic Portfolio Choice in Retirement." *Journal of Pension Economics and Finance* 9 (April), pp. 163–83.

Investment Company Institute (ICI). 2010. *The U.S. Retirement Market.* Washington (www.ici.org/pdf/fm-v19n3-a1.pd).

Lachance, Marie-Eve, and Olivia S. Mitchell. 2003. "Understanding Individual Account Guarantees." *American Economic Review Papers and Proceedings* 93, no. 2 (May), pp. 257–60.

Lachance, Marie-Eve, Olivia S. Mitchell, and Kent Smetters. 2003. "Guaranteeing Defined Contribution Pensions: The Option to Buy Back a Defined Benefit Promise." *Journal of Risk and Insurance* 70, no. 1, pp. 1–16.

Lusardi, Annamaria, and Olivia S. Mitchell. 2007a. "Baby Boomer Retirement Security: The Roles of Planning, Financial Literacy, and Housing Wealth." *Journal of Monetary Economics* 54, no. 1 (January), pp. 205–24.

———. 2007b. "Financial Literacy and Retirement Preparedness. Evidence and Implications for Financial Education." *Business Economics* (January), pp. 35–44.

———. 2008. "Planning and Financial Literacy: How Do Women Fare?" *American Economic Review Papers and Proceedings* 98, no. 2, pp. 413–17.

Lusardi, Annamaria, Olivia S. Mitchell, and Vilsa Curto. 2010. "Financial Literacy among the Young: Evidence and Implications for Consumer Policy." *Journal of Consumer Affairs* 44, no. 2, pp. 358–80.

Madrian, Brigitte, and Dennis Shea. 2001. "The Power of Suggestion: Inertia in 401(k) Participation and Savings Behavior." *Quarterly Journal of Economics* 116 (4), pp. 1149–87.

Maurer, Raimond, Olivia S. Mitchell, and Ralph Rogalla. 2010. "The Effect of Uncertain Labor Income and Social Security on Lifecycle Portfolios." In *Reorienting Retirement Risk Management.* Oxford University Press.

McGill, Daniel, and others. 2004. *Fundamentals of Private Pensions,* 8th ed. Oxford University Press.

Mitchell, Olivia S. 2010a. "Implications of the Financial Crisis for Long-Run Retirement Security." Pension Research Council Working Paper WP2010-02.

———. 2010b. "Retirement Risk Management in Times of Turmoil." *Elder Law Journal* 17, no. 2, pp. 439–60.

Mitchell, Olivia S., John Piggott, and Noriyuke Takayama. 2011. *Revisiting Retirement Payouts: Market Developments and Policy Issues.* Oxford University Press. Forthcoming.

Mitchell, Olivia S., and John Turner. 2010. "Human Capital Risk and Pension Outcomes." In *Evaluating the Financial Performance of Pension Funds,* edited by Richard P. Hinz and others, pp. 119–51. Washington: World Bank.

Mitchell, Olivia S., James Poterba, and Mark J. Warshawsky. 1999. "New Evidence on the Money's Worth of Individual Annuities." *American Economic Review* 89 (5) (December), pp. 1299–1318.

Mitchell, Olivia S., and others. 2006. "Financial Innovations for an Aging World." In *Demography and Financial Markets,* edited by Christopher Kent, Anna Park, and Daniel Rees, pp. 299–336. Reserve Bank of Australia.

Mitchell, Olivia S., and others. 2009. "Default, Framing, and Spillover Effects: The Case of Lifecycle Funds in 401(k) Plans." NBER Working Paper 15108. Cambridge, Mass.: National Bureau of Economic Research.

Mitchell, Olivia S., and Stephen Utkus. 2004. "Lessons from Behavioral Finance for Retirement Plan Design." In *Pension Design and Structure: New Lessons from Behavioral Finance,* edited by Olivia S. Mitchell and Stephen P. Utkus. Oxford University Press.

Moore, Rebecca. 2010. "Global Retirement Assets See Growth in 2009," June 25 (www.plansponsor.com/Global_Retirement_Assets_See_Growth_in_2009.aspx).

Munnell, Alicia H., and Annika Sundén. 2004. *Coming Up Short: The Challenge of 401(k) Plans.* Washington: Brookings.

Nishiyama, Kengo, and Hiroshi Nakanishi. 2010. "Japan's Ticking Pension Time Bomb: Underfunded Corporate Retirement Portfolios Could Have Big Consequences for the Market." *Wall Street Journal,* September 14 (http://online.wsj.com/article/SB10001424052748703466704575489120297253054.html).

Nomura, Akiko. 2009. "Proposal for Fundamentally Reforming Japan's Defined Contribution Pensions." *Nomura Journal of Capital Markets* 1, no. 3 (November 19).

OECD. 2010. *Pension Markets in Focus.* July (www.oecd.org/daf/pensions/pensionmarkets).

Shoven, John, and Sylvester Schieber. 1999. *The Real Deal: The History and Future of Social Security.* Yale University Press.

Smetters, Kent A. 2004. "Trading with the Unborn: A New Perspective on Capital Income Taxation." Working Paper 066. University of Michigan, Michigan Retirement Research Center.

Tang, Ning, and Olivia S. Mitchell. 2010. "Trading Behavior of 401(k) Pension Plan Participants in Times of Financial Turmoil." Pension Research Council Working Paper. University of Pennsylvania, Wharton School.

Tang, Ning, and others. 2010 "The Efficiency of Sponsor and Participant Portfolio Choices in 401(k) Plans." *Journal of Public Economics* 94, pp. 1073–85.

Thaler, Richard, and Shlomo Benartzi. 2004. "Save More Tomorrow: Using Behavioral Economics to Increase Employee Saving." *Journal of Political Economy* 112, no. 1 (February), pp. S164-S187.

Towers Watson. 2010. *The 2010 Global Pension Assets Study.* January www.towerswatson.com/research/972.

Vanguard Group. 2010. *Behavior of DC Plan Participants during Recent Market Volatility.* Valley Forge, Penn.

Webb, Anthony, and Natalia Zhivan. 2010. "How Much Is Enough? The Distribution of Lifetime Health Care Costs." Center for Retirement Research WP 2010-1 (February).

ROBERT C. POZEN
BETSY PALMER
NATALIE SHAPIRO

5

Asset Allocation by Institutional Investors after the Recent Financial Crisis

ASSET ALLOCATION IS THE KEY to the long-term performance of institutional investors; it has determined more than 90 percent of their performance over several decades.[1] For example, if an institutional investor held a diversified portfolio of U.S. stocks from 1991 to 1999, it would have recorded excellent performance regardless of the individual stocks selected. Conversely, that institution would have recorded relatively poor performance from 2000 to 2008 if it held a diversified portfolio of U.S. stocks regardless of the individual stocks selected.

By asset allocation, we mean the division of an institution's capital among a variety of asset classes in accordance with the institution's long-term policy goals. The asset categories may be fairly broad, such as stocks, bonds, alternative investments, and cash. Alternatively, they may be fairly specific, such as U.S. stocks, non-U.S. stocks, government bonds, corporate bonds, hedge funds, private equity, and real estate.

This type of long-term asset allocation should be distinguished from tactical asset allocation. Strategic asset allocation is aimed at fulfilling an institutional investor's policy goals over a full market cycle lasting at least five to ten years. Tactical asset allocation is an attempt to take advantage of short-term opportunities

---

1. Brinson, Hood, and Beebower (1986); Brinson, Singer, and Beebower (1991).

in the market when certain asset categories appear to be out of line with economic fundamentals. Tactical asset allocation may be performed quarterly, monthly, or even daily.[2]

This chapter examines strategic asset allocations by institutional investors globally after the financial crisis of 2008 to 2009, focusing on changes in asset allocation by corporate and government defined benefit (DB) pension plans, foundations, and university endowments.[3] These institutional investors have considerable discretion in setting their asset allocations. By contrast, changes in asset allocations by mutual funds, defined contribution (DC) plans, and brokerage accounts are directed primarily by their retail customers and their advisers.

The first part of the chapter delineates the main trends in asset allocation from 2007 to 2009 by institutional investors in various geographic areas—the United States, Europe, Canada, the United Kingdom, Japan, and Asia excluding Japan (hereafter referred to as Asia). The key trends include

—decreased allocation to equities (together with a shift from home country to global equities)

—increased allocation to fixed income

—increased allocation to alternative investments.

The second part evaluates these key trends in asset allocation in light of the policy objectives apparently driving them. The shift from domestic to global equities will probably fulfill the objective of more diversification of risk for institutional investors. While the shift from equities in the aggregate to high-quality bonds is likely to reduce portfolio volatility from year to year, that shift entails more interest rate risk, especially in the current environment of historically low rates. The sharp rise in institutional allocations to alternative investments does not appear likely to meet the objective of consistently positive returns in all market environments, though alternatives are likely to be less volatile on a year-to-year basis than stocks or possibly bonds.

The third part of the chapter analyzes in depth the factors influencing asset allocation decisions by specific types of institutional investors—DB pension plans of S&P 500 companies, DB pension plans of state and local governments, and investment funds of foundations and endowments. Because of limits on data availability, these analyses are confined to institutional investors within the United States. In an effort to "de-risk" their portfolios, corporate DB plans are moving allocations from stocks to bonds. However, as explained above, those plans

2. Anson (2004).
3. This chapter sometimes refers to "institutional investors" as "investors."

may be taking on considerable interest rate risk at the wrong point in the cycle. If interest rates rise, the value of their bond portfolios will be reduced, although their projected liabilities also will decrease. By contrast, public pension plans are taking a more aggressive stance by concentrating heavily on international equities and alternative investments. Although that approach can be explained by the large funding deficits faced by many public plans, those plans run a substantial risk of not meeting their ambitious goals for investment returns. Last, endowments and foundations also are poised to expand their already heavy reliance on alternative investments, including hedge funds, private equity, and real estate. However, it is unclear whether alternative investments will meet their stated objective of absolute returns in the future since they failed to do so during the financial crisis.

Geographic Trends in Asset Allocation

Institutional investors around the world have shifted their investment asset allocations in the aftermath of the global stock market meltdown. While allocations to various asset classes remained relatively stable from 2005 to 2006, shifts began to emerge by 2007. Not all regions started with the same baseline for asset allocation in 2007. For instance, investors in Europe traditionally have had much lower allocations to equities than those in the United States. Similarly, not all shifts in asset allocation are parallel across regions. Nevertheless, some common themes emerge among institutional investors globally, including reducing exposure to equities, especially domestic equities; increasing fixed-income allocations; and generally increasing allocations to alternative investments such as hedge funds, private equity, and real estate. While adjustments to portfolio asset allocation (calculated using market values) may have been a direct result of sharply declining equities during the stock market crash of 2008 and early 2009, thus far the data do not suggest that investors are looking to rebalance back to pre-crash allocations among asset categories.

Declining Equity Allocations

Institutional investors have reduced their exposure to equities since 2007, and investors in the United Kingdom and the United States have undertaken the steepest reductions. In the United States, the equity allocation dropped from 59.6 percent in 2007 to 47.3 percent in 2009. Even regions with historically low preferences for equities (Japan and Asia) have reduced equity exposure over the past two years (figure 5-1).

Figure 5-1. *Equity (All) Asset Allocation across Regions, 2005–09*

Percent of total assets

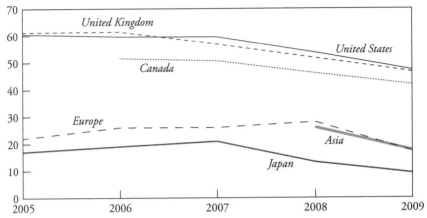

Source: Greenwich Associates Surveys, 2005–09. Proprietary subscriber commissioned surveys. Data used with permission.

Looking at the exposure more closely, the prevailing trend in every region around the world has been to reduce exposure to domestic equities (figure 5-2).[4] In some regions, the allocation away from domestic equities started before 2007 and continued through 2009. For example, according to survey results, institutional investors in the United States allocated nearly 47 percent of their assets to U.S. equities in 2005, but by 2009 they had allocated only 32 percent. Analysis of institutional asset data shows that net flows by institutional investors to U.S. equities have been negative since 2007.[5]

U.K. institutions have demonstrated a similar sharp fall-off in allocations to U.K. equities, from 34 percent in 2005 to 19 percent in 2009. While Japanese institutional investors traditionally have not allocated a high percentage of their portfolios to equities, even their allocation to domestic equities dropped from 11 percent to 6 percent between 2005 and 2009.

With global stocks off 50 percent in 2008, it is not surprising that equities became a smaller part of institutional allocations. Since institutional portfolios are

4. While the timing of surveys addressing asset allocation varies by region—that is, in some regions the results reflect responses given at the beginning of the year and in other regions the surveys were conducted closer to the end of the year—the general trend away from domestic equities was consistent globally over the 2005–09 period.

5. Casey, Quirk & Associates (2010, Executive Summary, p. 1).

Figure 5-2. *Domestic Equity Asset Allocation across Regions, 2005–09*

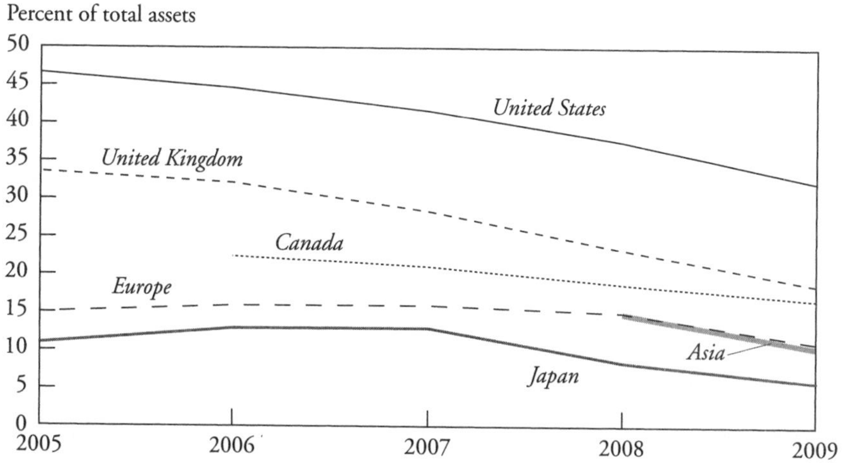

Percent of total assets

Source: Greenwich Associates Surveys, 2005–09. Proprietary subscriber commissioned surveys. Data used with permission.

measured by market values, equity allocations should have dropped by 50 percent from March 2008 to March 2009, all else being equal. Nevertheless, it is reasonable to assume that institutional investors, with considerable expertise and resources at their disposal, would have rebalanced their portfolios to reflect their policy objectives at the end of 2009. Those policy objectives seemed to have called for lower equity allocations before 2008, although that trend was accelerated by the market crash. At the end of 2009, institutional investors either did not rebalance back to their previous target allocations or altered their targets because the decline was taking them in the direction that they wanted to go anyway.

Survey data from 2009 regarding intentions with respect to asset allocation going forward indicate a continued preference for reducing home country equity exposure in the United States, Canada, the United Kingdom, and Japan. When respondents were asked whether they expected to significantly increase or decrease their exposure to home country equities over the next three years, institutional investors in these four regions who expected to reduce their exposure far out-numbered those who expected to increase their exposure (figures 5-3 and 5-4). (In these figures and other survey data regarding investors' intentions, the label "active" refers to actively managed strategies and the term "passive" refers to passively managed strategies. An active manager makes investments with the goal of outperforming an investment benchmark index; a passive manager seeks to

Figure 5-3. *United States and Canada, Domestic Equity:*
Expectations of Future Asset Allocation

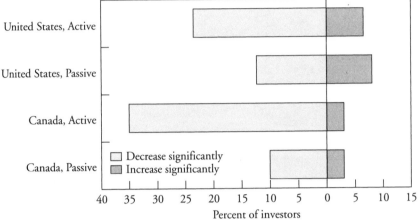

Source: Greenwich Associates Survey, 2009. Proprietary subscriber commissioned survey. Data used with permission.

Figure 5-4. *United Kingdom and Japan, Domestic Equity:*
Expectations of Future Asset Allocation

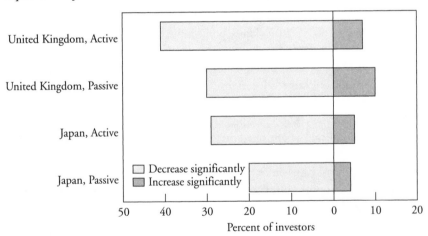

Source: Greenwich Associates Survey, 2009. Proprietary subscriber commissioned survey. Data used with permission.

Figure 5-5. *Europe and Asia, Domestic Equity: Expectations of Future Asset Allocation*

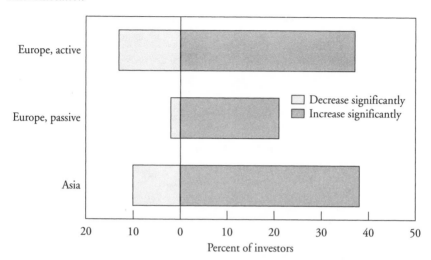

Source: Greenwich Associates Survey, 2009. Proprietary subscriber commissioned survey. Data used with permission.

replicate the investment weightings and returns of an index.) However, in Asia and Europe, survey results reveal a preference for a higher allocation to domestic equities (figure 5-5). A preference for increased domestic equity exposure in Asia and Europe also was revealed in 2010 survey results.[6] In the case of Europe, exposure to domestic equities historically has been low, so the expected increase is off a modest base. In Asia, enthusiasm for economic growth prospects in the region may be fueling the continued appeal of domestic equities.

With respect to allocations to international and global equities, the picture is more mixed (figure 5-6). After 2005, allocations across regions generally rose, but that trend was disrupted by the market crash. For example, exposure to international/global stocks for U.S.-based investors increased from 13.9 percent in 2005 to 17.9 percent in 2007. Yet by 2009, the aggregate exposure for U.S. institutions had fallen back to 15.1 percent, only slightly greater than the exposure in 2005. More recently, asset flows have been directed to international/global equities. According to an analysis of eVestment Alliance data by Casey, Quirk & Associates in the first quarter of 2010, "Non-U.S. equity products continue to be the beneficiaries of new asset flows as investors seek global diversification."[7]

6. Greenwich Associates (2010a).
7. Casey, Quirk & Associates (2010, p. 7).

Figure 5-6. *International/Global Equity Asset Allocation across Regions, 2005–09*

Percent of total assets

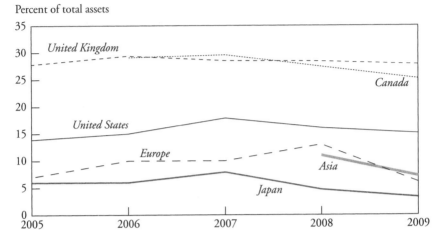

Source: Greenwich Associates Surveys, 2005–09. Proprietary subscriber commissioned surveys. Data used with permission.

Exposure to international/global stocks outside their home country for U.K. investors has been relatively consistent at around 28 percent since 2005. Investors in the United Kingdom therefore appear to have rebalanced their portfolios in favor of international/global stocks after the market crash of 2008–09. International/global allocation by Asian institutions declined to about 7 percent in 2009, where it currently remains.[8] In 2009 the allocation for European investors dropped sharply, to 6.5 percent, but subsequently partially rebounded to 10.5 percent, suggesting that rebalancing had occurred.[9]

With respect to intentions regarding exposure to international/global stocks, in the United States, Canada, Europe, and Asia, more investors said that they were looking to "significantly increase" than to "significantly decrease" exposure (figures 5-7 and 5-8). That appears to be a continuation of the trend that was interrupted by the stock market crash. In addition to the potential for diversification, there is growing recognition among investors that globalization supports the argument in favor of investing outside of one's own country. Because industries compete with one another in a global economy, the best investment opportunities may lie elsewhere.

8. Greenwich Associates (2010b).
9. Greenwich Associates (2010c).

Figure 5-7. *United States and Canada, International/Global Equity:*
Expectations of Future Asset Allocation

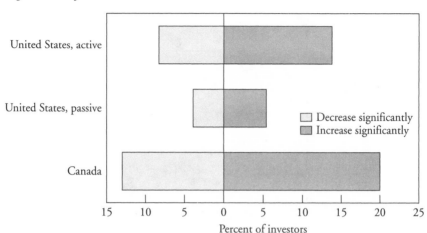

Source: Greenwich Associates Survey, 2009. Proprietary subscriber commissioned survey. Data used
with permission.

Figure 5-8. *Europe and Asia, International/Global Equity: Expectations of*
Future Asset Allocation

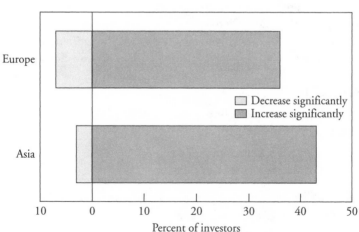

Source: Greenwich Associates Survey, 2009. Proprietary subscriber commissioned survey. Data used
with permission.

Figure 5-9. *United Kingdom and Japan, International/Global Equity: Expectations of Future Asset Allocation*

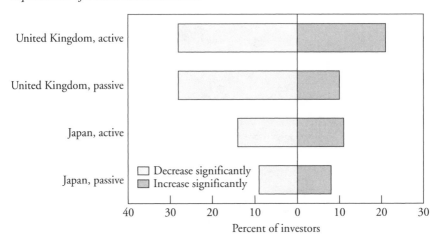

Source: Greenwich Associates Survey, 2009. Proprietary subscriber commissioned survey. Data used with permission.

However, the trend toward global diversification is not universal. Greenwich Associates concludes that although state and local government plans within the United States are increasing international/global allocations, U.S. corporate defined benefit plans are still looking to reduce exposure to global and international equities overall, in line with their primary objective of continuing to de-risk their plans.[10] In the United Kingdom and Japan, more investors look to significantly decrease than to significantly increase their exposure to international/global equities (figure 5-9). In a trend that parallels that in the United States, U.K. corporate defined benefit plans expect to reduce international/global stock exposure while allocations to this asset category by local authorities are on the rise.[11]

Increasing Allocations to Fixed Income

A clear trend among investors globally is an increased preference for fixed-income investments (figure 5-10). Allocations to fixed-income investments by institutional investors remained relatively stable from 2005 until 2007 except in Europe, which posted a decline from 61 percent to 55 percent during that time period. After 2007,

10. Greenwich Associates (2009).
11. Greenwich Associates (2010d).

Figure 5-10. *Fixed-Income Asset Allocation across Regions, 2005–09*

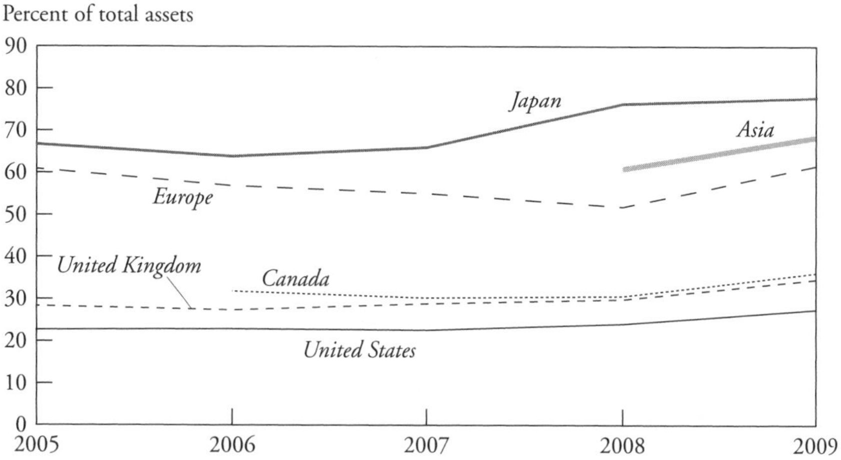

Percent of total assets

Source: Greenwich Associates Surveys, 2005–09. Proprietary subscriber commissioned surveys. Data used with permission.

allocations rose. For example, U.K. allocations rose from 29 percent in 2007 to 43 percent in 2009. In the United States, the allocation increased from 23 percent to 28 percent over the same period. That increase may have been at least in part market driven, since as stocks dropped globally, the overall percentage of better performing fixed-income assets increased. However, according to Casey, Quirk & Associates, there also was a "flight to safety by institutional investors in late 2008 and early 2009, when investors sought protection in fixed-income products as risk appetites diminished."[12]

That flight to safety is illustrated by significant purchases of U.S. Treasury securities by corporate and public plans. Data from the U.S. Federal Reserve Board indicate that from 2008 to 2009, outstanding public debt rose by 22 percent. Most of that increase was concentrated in instruments with one- to ten-year maturities. During the year, state and local government retirement funds increased their ownership of these securities by 19.2 percent, commensurate with the increase in supply. However, the rise in ownership by defined benefit corporate pension funds was 85.3 percent, more than four times that of the public funds.[13]

12. Casey, Quirk & Associates (2009, p. 5).
13. Board of Governors of the Federal Reserve System (2010).

Figure 5-11. *United States and Canada, Fixed Income: Expectations of Future Asset Allocation*

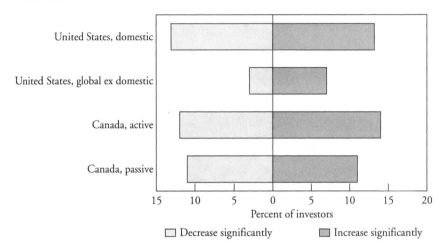

Percent of investors

☐ Decrease significantly   ▨ Increase significantly

Source: Greenwich Associates Survey, 2009. Proprietary subscriber commissioned survey. Data used with permission.

Institutional investors do not appear to have the significant exposure to fixed income outside their home country that they do to equities. That is not surprising because payout obligations of pension plans, university endowments, and other institutional investors usually are denominated in the local currency.[14]

Going forward, investors globally express a preference for higher allocations to fixed income. While surveys conducted by Greenwich Associates are framed differently by region (active/passive, domestic/global), the overall outlook is generally for more exposure to fixed income (figures 5-11, 5-12, and 5-13). That trend is especially pronounced outside the United States. Expectations of higher fixed-income allocations have been noted in other surveys, including an Institutional Investor Institute survey of clients in the United Kingdom and Europe. That survey found that 51 percent of the clients responding expected to

14. There may be structural reasons why U.S. corporate pension funds invest in bonds. Research by academic practitioners has highlighted the benefits of investing in bonds for corporate plans. Since income from bonds in pension plans is not taxed and a corporation gets tax deductions for the interest that it pays on bonds that it issues, a company can take advantage of different tax treatments by selling equities in the pension fund and buying bonds while issuing debt and buying back its own stock at the corporate level. However, that probably was not the motivation for higher allocations to fixed income after the crash of 2008–09. Instead, companies worried about their financial viability, increased their levels of cash, and refrained from share repurchases. Tepper (1981); Black (1980).

Figure 5-12. *United Kingdom and Europe, Fixed Income:*
Expectations of Future Asset Allocation

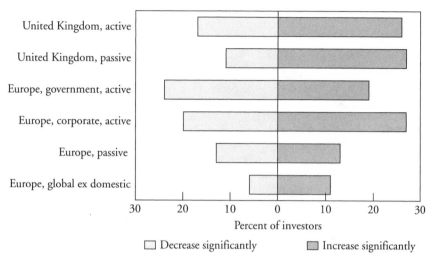

Source: Greenwich Associates Survey, 2009. Proprietary subscriber commissioned survey. Data used
with permission.

Figure 5-13. *Asia and Japan, Fixed Income: Expectations of Future Asset Allocation*

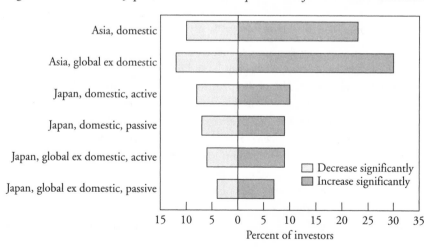

Source: Greenwich Associates Survey, 2009. Proprietary subscriber commissioned survey. Data used
with permission.

Figure 5-14. *Alternatives Asset Allocation across Regions, 2005–09*

Percent of total assets

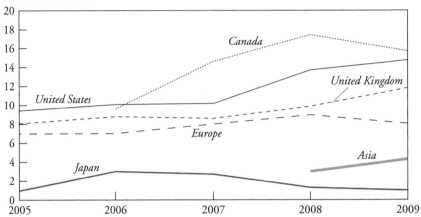

Source: Greenwich Associates Surveys, 2005–09. Proprietary subscriber commissioned surveys. Data used with permission.

increase their use of liability-driven investment (LDI) strategies, which typically involves heavy use of fixed-income strategies.[15] Higher allocations to fixed income may be a lasting impact of the crash as investors determine that they cannot withstand the volatility of equities in their portfolios.

Increasing Use of Alternatives

The last trend is an increase across most regions in the use of alternative invest-ments, including real estate, hedge funds, and private equity, albeit off a low base (figure 5-14). The one exception is Japan, where the use of these asset classes had risen to 3 percent in 2006 but fell back to only about 1 percent of asset allocation by 2009. In contrast, by 2009 the use of alternatives in the United States rose to nearly 15 percent from under 10 percent in 2005, and from 8 percent to about 12 percent in the United Kingdom.[16] Canadian investors also use alternative assets extensively (almost 16 percent in 2009), though exposure in 2008 was even higher. The trends in each of these three alternative asset classes are discussed separately below.

Figure 5-15 shows the trend for private equity investments by region. Histor-ically, private equity has not been a significant part of institutional portfolios in

15. Institutional Investor Institute (2010).
16. The term "alternatives" will sometimes be used for "alternative investments."

Figure 5-15. *Private Equity Asset Allocation across Regions, 2005–09*

Percent of total assets

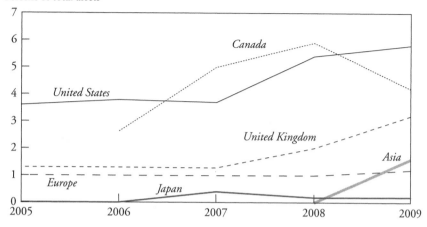

Source: Greenwich Associates Surveys, 2005–09. Proprietary subscriber commissioned surveys. Data used with permission.

general (with the exception of the endowment and foundation marketplace in the United States, discussed separately later in the chapter). The general allocation to this asset class appears to have been increasing since 2007. For example, survey results show that U.S. institutional investors reported a 5.8 percent allocation to private equity in 2009, up from 3.7 percent in 2007. However, because of the illiquidity of this asset class, returns for private equity typically are reported with a significant lag. Therefore, depending on the timing of the survey taken in 2009, the percentage of overall portfolio allocation that institutional investors reported may not fully reflect asset markdowns resulting from declining equity values in 2008.

Despite the illiquidity of private equity, institutional investors globally demonstrate interest in increasing their allocation to this asset class (figure 5-16). The 2009 Greenwich survey results across all regions show that more than 10 percent of those responding expressed their intent to significantly increase their exposure to private equity over the next three years. In Asia, half of all investors responding noted their intention to "significantly increase" their allocation. (Survey data for 2010 still show institutional investors in Asia favoring continued increases in private equity allocations, although the percentage declined to 23 percent.)[17]

17. Greenwich Associates (2010b).

Figure 5-16. *Private Equity, All Regions: Expectations of Future Asset Allocation*

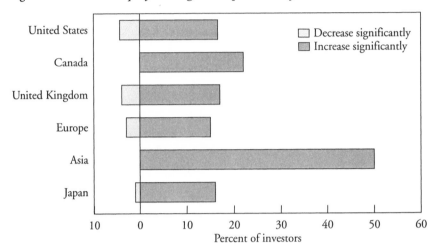

Source: Greenwich Associates Survey, 2009. Proprietary subscriber commissioned survey. Data used with permission.

This broad-based preference for private equity seems inconsistent with two other trends. First, the illiquidity of private equity proved to be a challenge for certain institutional investors during the credit crisis of 2008–09. Perhaps this characteristic of private equity was counterbalanced by the high liquidity of investment-grade bonds, allocations to which were increased by many institutional investors. Second, profitable exits by private equity managers, whether through the public markets or to private buyers, depend heavily on a robust market for publicly traded equities—an asset category to which most institutions reduced their allocations over the past few years. Perhaps investors counted on an episodic surge in the initial public offering (IPO) market despite pessimism about long-term equity returns.

With respect to hedge funds, allocations by U.S. and U.K. investors have steadily risen since 2005, again from a very low base. By contrast, investors in Asia and Japan report declining commitments to hedge funds, and in 2009 they reported that less than 1 percent of their assets were allocated to this asset class (figure 5-17). Based on 2009 expectations data, however, in every region except Europe more respondents indicated they would significantly increase rather than significantly decrease their hedge fund exposure (figure 5-18). In the United States, for example, 15 percent reported that they expect to significantly increase their exposure

Figure 5-17. *Hedge Funds Asset Allocation across Regions, 2005–09*

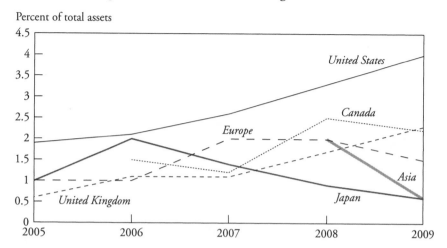

Percent of total assets

Source: Greenwich Associates Surveys, 2005–09. Proprietary subscriber commissioned surveys. Data used with permission.

Figure 5-18. *Hedge Funds, All Regions: Expectations of Future Asset Allocation*

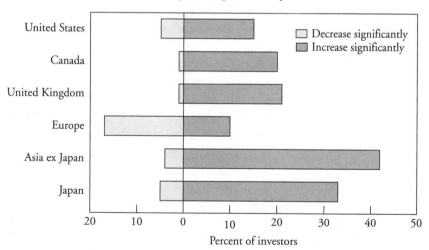

Percent of investors

Source: Greenwich Associates Survey, 2009. Proprietary subscriber commissioned survey. Data used with permission.

Figure 5-19. *Real Estate Asset Allocation across Regions, 2005–09*

Percent of total assets

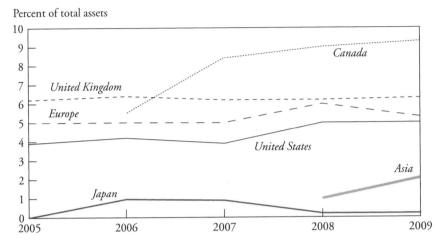

Source: Greenwich Associates Surveys, 2005–09. Proprietary subscriber commissioned surveys. Data used with permission.

while 5 percent reported that they would significantly decrease exposure. In Asia, 42 percent of respondents reported their intention to significantly increase exposure while only 4 percent expected to significantly decrease exposure. However, 2010 survey results indicate that enthusiasm for hedge funds among investors in Asia has waned. The percentage of respondents expecting to increase their exposure to hedge funds (18 percent) was about the same as that of those expecting to decrease exposure (19 percent).[18]

Last, allocations to real estate have remained fairly consistent since 2005 for many regions, including the United Kingdom, at about 6 percent, and the United States, at 4 percent to 5 percent. Canadian investors, however, increased allocations to real estate from 5.5 percent in 2006 to more than 9 percent by 2009 (figure 5-19). Here again, global investors surveyed reported far more interest in significantly increasing than in significantly decreasing exposure to this asset class over the next three years (figure 5-20). According to 2009 survey results, 38 percent of investors in Asia said that they would significantly increase their exposure while only 10 percent said that they would significantly decrease exposure. In the United States, 12 percent said that they would significantly increase and 4 percent said that they would significantly decrease their exposure. Canadians,

18. Greenwich Associates (2010a).

Figure 5-20. *Real Estate, All Regions: Expectations of Future Asset Allocation*

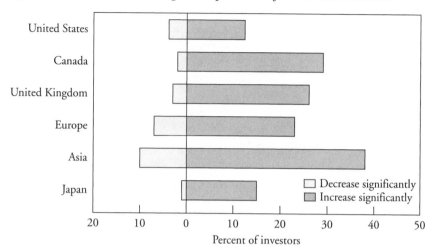

Source: Greenwich Associates Survey, 2009. Proprietary subscriber commissioned survey. Data used with permission.

who already have more assets committed to this asset class than institutional investors in other regions, continue to express robust interest in increasing their exposure (29 percent versus only 2 percent who expect to significantly decrease exposure). The 2010 survey results report that investors in the United Kingdom, Europe, and Asia also indicated a continued preference for adding to their real estate exposure.[19]

Evaluation of Three Main Trends in Asset Allocation

As mentioned, there were three trends in asset allocation among institutional investors throughout the world (with a few exceptions):

—decrease in overall allocation to equities (with more of the equity allocation going to global equities and less to home country equities)

—increase in fixed income (with emphasis on government and high-quality corporate bonds)

—increase in alternative investments (including hedge funds, private equity funds, and real estate).

19. Greenwich Associates (2010a). Greenwich Associates data for 2010 for other regions were unavailable at the time of this writing.

These trends can be viewed together as one overarching shift in asset allocation by institutional investors: swapping out of equities (especially domestic stocks) into a combination of high-quality bonds and alternative investments. The policy objectives behind this trade seemed twofold: immunizing the liabilities of institutional investors while generating higher returns with less volatility. Here we evaluate these three asset allocation trends in light of the policy objectives apparently driving these changes.

Diversification among Asset Categories and within Equities Was Well Supported

Before the financial crisis of 2008–09, it often was taken for granted that diversification among asset categories had a beneficial impact on the risk/return relationship of an institutional investor's securities portfolio. The benefits of diversification by asset class were readily apparent over the long term, with negative correlations among stocks and most types of bonds. Correlations among U.S., non-U.S., and emerging market equities as well as high-yield bonds historically have been positive but nevertheless have provided investors with some diversification benefits (table 5-1).

But the conventional wisdom was thrown into doubt by the convergence of returns among asset classes during the 2008–09 financial crisis. The returns of all asset categories plummeted, with the exception of U.S. Treasuries and other sovereign bonds from advanced industrial countries, which became safe havens for investors. From April 1, 2008, through March 31, 2009, correlations among nearly all asset categories increased markedly (table 5-2).

That phenomenon of highly correlated returns among asset categories turned out to be short-lived. Within one year after the financial crisis, correlations among asset categories decreased significantly, though they were still higher than they had been over the last decade (table 5-3). Thus, the benefits of diversification across all asset categories generally were realized by institutional investors if they were prepared to take a long-term approach to the positioning of their portfolios.

In particular, institutional investors that moved away from home country equities to a portfolio of more global equities did reap the benefits of diversification over the long term. For example, the correlation between the S&P 500 Stock Index and the MSCI World Ex US Index, which was 0.83 for the ten years ended December 31, 2007, rose to 0.94 during the twelve months ended March 31, 2009, and fell back to 0.88 in the twelve months ended March 31, 2010. Similarly, the correlation between the S&P 500 and the MSCI Emerging Market Equity Index, which was 0.72 for the ten years ended December 31, 2007, rose to 0.89 during the twelve months ended March 31, 2009, and fell back to 0.83 for the twelve months ended March 31, 2010.

Table 5-1. *Correlation Matrix for the Ten Years Ended December 2007, Monthly Return Data*

Source	S&P 500	MSCI World ex United States	Emerging Markets Equity	Barclays Aggregate	Barclays High Yield	Barclays 3–5 Year Treasury	Barclays Long Treasury
S&P 500	1.00						
MSCI World ex United States	0.83	1.00					
Emerging Markets Equity	0.72	0.78	1.00				
Barclays Aggregate	−0.22	−0.19	−0.22	1.00			
Barclays High Yield	0.49	0.49	0.53	0.07	1.00		
Barclays 3–5 Year Treasury	−0.34	−0.32	−0.33	0.93	−0.18	1.00	
Barclays Long Treasury	−0.29	−0.25	−0.28	0.94	−0.03	0.87	1.00

Sources: Datastream, Standard & Poor's, MSCI BARRA, and Barclays Capital, available to subscribers at www.datastream.com.

Table 5-2. *Correlation Matrix April 2008 through March 2009, Monthly Return Data*

Source	S&P 500	MSCI World ex United States	Emerging Markets Equity	Barclays Aggregate	Barclays High Yield	Barclays 3–5 Year Treasury	Barclays Long Treasury
S&P 500	1.00						
MSCI World ex US	0.94	1.00					
Emerging Markets Equity	0.89	0.96	1.00				
Barclays Aggregate	0.46	0.61	0.55	1.00			
Barclays High Yield	0.71	0.78	0.82	0.38	1.00		
Barclays 3–5 Year Treasury	−0.20	−0.21	−0.28	0.50	−0.52	1.00	
Barclays Long Treasury	0.28	0.37	0.28	0.87	−0.05	0.75	1.00

Sources: Datastream, Standard & Poor's, MSCI BARRA, and Barclays Capital, available to subscribers at www.datastream.com.

Table 5-3. *Correlation Matrix April 2009 through March 2010, Monthly Return Data*

Source	S&P 500	MSCI World ex United States	Emerging Markets Equity	Barclays Aggregate	Barclays High Yield	Barclays 3–5 Year Treasury	Barclays Long Treasury
S&P 500	1.00						
MSCI World ex United States	0.88	1.00					
Emerging Markets Equity	0.83	0.94	1.00				
Barclays Aggregate	0.04	0.04	−0.04	1.00			
Barclays High Yield	0.65	0.81	0.84	0.00	1.00		
Barclays 3–5 Year Treasury	−0.23	−0.36	−0.41	0.84	−0.45	1.00	
Barclays Long Treasury	−0.33	−0.46	−0.53	0.76	−0.54	0.88	1.00

Sources: Datastream, Standard & Poor's, MSCI BARRA, and Barclays Capital, available to subscribers at www.datastream.com.

Investors outside the United States also benefited from diversification beyond their home country over the long term. The correlation between Japanese equities and the MSCI World Ex Japan Index was 0.49 for the ten-year period ended December 2007. During the height of the crisis (the one-year period ended March 2009), it rose to 0.94. In the twelve subsequent months, however, correlations declined to 0.68, still above the long-term average but lower than during the peak of the crisis. The pattern of correlations was repeated for U.K. investors, although to a far more muted extent. For the ten-year period ended in 2007, the correlation between U.K. equities and stocks outside the United Kingdom was 0.87. The correlation rose to 0.93 for the one-year period ended in March 2009 and subsequently declined to 0.90.[20]

In short, the move away from home country equities to a more global portfolio of securities made sense for institutional investors globally. While correlations converged during the crisis, they moved back toward long-term relationships in the year after the crisis. In addition to the benefits of diversification, expanding the opportunity set to include global equities allows investors to take advantage of attractive opportunities in emerging or other developed markets.

Shift to Fixed Income Was Understandable but Short-Sighted

As the equity portfolios of institutional investors shifted from a home country to a global basis, their overall equity positions declined in favor of fixed income after the financial crisis. That decline appeared to be a result partly of the decision to move to the safety of high-quality debt and partly of the steep drop in the market value of equities in the year before March 2009.

During the financial crisis, liquidity in the securities markets declined sharply. To achieve higher levels of liquidity, many investors shifted assets to government bonds during the crisis. For example, institutional investors moved large sums out of money market funds holding commercial paper into those holding only U.S. government paper.

This dramatic decline in liquidity during the financial crisis had a significant impact on certain institutional investors. For example, some university endowments were hard pressed to meet their funding obligations to sponsors of private equity funds, and other pension plans were challenged to meet their payout requirements. Again, it is quite understandable that those institutions favored government bonds, with their high degree of liquidity.

---

20. Correlations calculated using FactSet Research System's SPAR application using monthly returns of regional indexes; data available to subscribers at www.factset.com.

Table 5-4. *Risk and Return for Various Asset Classes, 2009–10*
Percent

Source	Return	Risk[a]
Twelve Months ended March 2009		
S&P 500	−38.1	25.9
MSCI World ex United States	−46.0	29.4
Barclays 3–5 Year Treasury	6.8	5.4
Barclays Long Treasury	13.1	19.5
Twelve months ended March 2010		
S&P 500	49.8	13.3
MSCI World ex US	56.8	19.6
Barclays 3–5 Year Treasury	0.6	3.9
Barclays Long Treasury	−7.3	9.6

Sources: Datastream, Standard & Poor's, MSCI BARRA, and Barclays Capital, available to subscribers at www.datastream.com.

a. Risk is measured by the standard deviation of returns: the greater the standard deviation, the greater the volatility or risk.

Government bonds also offered high returns with lower risk than equities during the peak of the financial crisis. In the twelve months ended March 31, 2009, the returns of the Barclays Long U.S. Treasury Index and the Barclays 3-5 Year U.S. Treasury Index were 13.1 percent and 6.8 percent respectively, with volatility of 19.5 percent and 5.4 percent respectively. By contrast, for the twelve months ended March 31, 2009, the S&P 500 and the MSCI World Ex-US Index returned −38.1 percent and −46.0 percent respectively, with volatility of 25.9 percent and 29.4 percent respectively (table 5-4).

However, those outstanding returns for U.S. government bonds were short-lived. During the twelve months ended March 31, 2010, the return and risk for the Barclays Long Term U.S. Treasury Index were −7.3 percent and 9.6 percent respectively, while the return and risk of the Barclays 3–5 year U.S. Treasury Index were 0.6 percent and 3.9 percent respectively. By contrast, during the twelve months ended March 31, 2010, the return and risk of the S&P 500 Index were 49.8 percent and 13.3 percent respectively, while the return and risk of the MSCI World Ex US Index were 56.8 percent and 19.6 percent respectively (table 5-4).

Of course, it is difficult to predict the risk-return ratios of asset categories over the next five to ten years. However, the low interest rates offered by ten-year U.S. Treasuries during 2009—between 2.2 percent and 4.0 percent—were insufficient to meet the return assumptions required by many pension plans to avoid further contributions. Return assumptions for most pension plans have continued to hover close to 8 percent despite strong evidence that those assumptions are not realistic (figure 5-21).

Moreover, by increasing their holdings in long-term government bonds during 2009, institutional investors were implicitly taking on considerable interest rate risk over the next five to ten years. Consider figure 5-22, which shows interest rate levels for five- and ten-year U.S. Treasury bonds since 1960. This figure demonstrates that long-term interest rates were at historic lows in 2009 and 2010, so they are more likely to rise than fall over the next five to ten years (absent deflation). If long-term interest rates rise, the bond portfolios of institutional investors will fall in value. But that fall may be offset to some degree by the decrease in projected liabilities of public and private pension plans. The present values of the pension plans' obligations are heavily influenced by long-term interest rates.

Increase in Alternative Investments

Institutional investors generally increased their allocations to alternative investments, including hedge funds and private equity funds. In making such investments, institutional investors generally were seeking absolute returns rather than relative returns. A manager promising absolute returns should deliver positive results even in down markets, often by taking significant short positions. By contrast, a traditional long manager seeks to achieve superior relative performance—higher returns than the relevant benchmark. For example, a long-only strategy would be considered successful if it declined 5 percent when the benchmark declined 7 percent.

Although the managers of hedge funds promised absolute returns, hedge funds on average had large negative returns (−19 percent) in 2008.[21] Yet institutional investors still allocated more to hedge funds during 2009, when, on average, they had positive returns of +20 percent—much lower than the return of global equities (+35 percent) in 2009 (table 5-5). The appeal of hedge funds most likely stems from the lower volatility and diversification benefit of the asset class, in addition to return potential.

Even that possible explanation of increased institutional allocations to hedge funds may be based on overstated performance results. Several studies have shown that average hedge fund returns were overstated by approximately 3 percent a year due to survivorship bias.[22] Survivorship bias occurs when a failed fund is removed from a database along with its performance history. Similarly, several

21. Hedge Fund Research Index (www.hedgefundresearch.com).
22. Brown, Goetzmann, and Ibbotson (1999); Fung and Hsieh (2000).

Figure 5-21. *Pension Plans' Return Assumptions*

Panel A: Expected Investment Return Rates for Public Pension Plans
Number of plans reporting

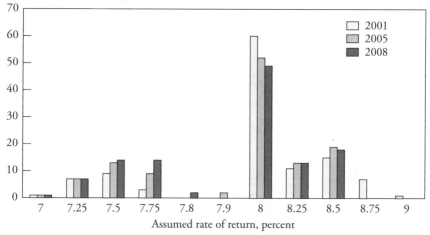

Assumed rate of return, percent

Panel B: Changes to Return Assumptions Reported by S&P 500 Companies with Pension Plans
Number of S&P 500 companies

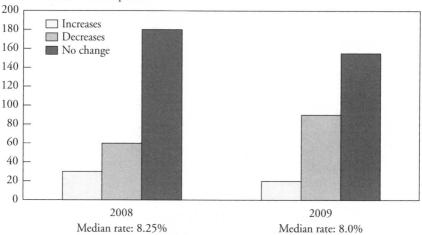

Sources: National Association of State Retirement Administrators; "Analyst's Accounting Observer," *Wall Street Journal,* September 18–19, 2010 (www.wsjonline.com).

Figure 5-22. *U.S. Treasury Bond Interest Rates, 1960–2010*

Percent

Source: Board of Governors of the Federal Reserve System (www.federalreserve.org).

Table 5-5. *Hedge Fund Returns versus Other Equity Indices, Annual Periods*[a]
Percent

Source	2008	2009
Hedge Fund Index	−19.03	19.98
S&P 500 Index	−37.45	25.55
MSCI AC World Index	−42.19	34.63

Source: HFRI (hedge fund data at www.hedgefundresearch.com), Standard & Poor's, and MSCI BARRA.

a. Returns are constructed from over 2,000 self-reported hedge fund manager returns. Returns are net of all fees, and the index is equal weighted.

studies have estimated that average returns of hedge funds are overstated by at least 2 percent a year due to backfill bias. Backfill bias occurs when hedge funds are selective about whether to include prior return history when they begin reporting returns to databases. Hedge funds typically include historical data only when returns have been good. Such selective reporting of the most favorable start date for returns therefore tends to elevate the overall level of hedge fund returns in the databases.[23]

23. Malkiel and Saha (2005); Posthuma and Van der Sluis (2003).

Table 5-6. *Private Equity Returns versus Other Equity Indices, Annual Periods*
Percent

Item	March 31, 2008	March 31, 2009	March 31, 2010
Private equity	11.45	−23.86	22.35
S&P 500 Index	−5.08	−38.09	49.77
Russell 2000 Index	−13.00	−37.50	62.76

Source: Cambridge Associates (private equity data at www.cambridgeassociates.com), Standard & Poor's, and Frank Russell Company.

In any event, we do know that fees are coming down for hedge funds and funds of hedge funds. In 2007, the norm for funds of hedge funds was a 1 percent base fee and a performance fee of 10 percent of realized gains. In 2009, the average performance fee for funds of hedge funds fell to 6.5 percent of realized gains, according to Eurekahedge, a data provider.[24] Similarly, institutional investors have been pressuring hedge funds to lower their fees—originally 2 percent (base fee) + 20 percent (performance fee paid on realized gains)—which had crept up to 2 percent + 30 percent, 3 percent + 20 percent, and even 3 percent + 30 percent.[25]

The objective of most private equity funds differed from that of most hedge funds. Most private equity funds aim to deliver returns 4 percent to 5 percent above those generated by a broad-base stock index like the S&P 500 over five- to ten-year periods. But private equity funds do not promise positive returns every year, since their profitable exits depend heavily on strong equity markets. Indeed, during the past few years, the return pattern has mimicked that of hedge funds— that is, not as bad during the down period but not as good during the upswing. Table 5-6 shows the mean private equity manager return compared with the returns for the S&P 500 and the Russell 2000 Stock Small-Cap Index for three recent annual time periods.

On a longer-term basis, Kaplan and Schoar showed that the average returns of private equity funds, after all fees, matched or slightly underperformed the S&P 500 Index from 1980 through 2001.[26] Similar research by Phalippou and Gottschalg contends that private equity funds, after fees, underperformed the S&P 500 by 3 percent a year from 1980 to 2003.[27] On the other hand, independent studies by three firms, Cambridge Associates, Venture Economics

24. Eurekahedge (www.eurekahedge.com).
25. De Sa'Pinto (2010).
26. Kaplan and Schoar (2005).
27. Phalippou and Gottschalg (2005).

Figure 5-23. *Private Equity Historical Performance*[a]

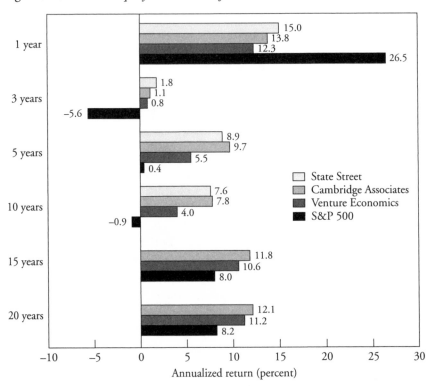

Annualized return (percent)

Sources: State Street, Cambridge Associates, Venture Economics, JP Morgan Asset Management. JP Morgan Asset Management Report, "Private Equity: Exploring the Full Equity Spectrum," November 2009. Updated December 31, 2009.

a. Time-weighted annualized returns for periods ending December 31, 2009. Median returns net to investors.

(Thomson Reuters), and State Street, conclude that although private equity funds underperformed the S&P 500 in 2009, they outperformed over three-, five-, ten-, fifteen- and twenty-year periods ended December 31, 2009 (figure 5-23).

Yet there is a general consensus that the returns of the top quartile of private equity managers are significantly better than those of the other private equity managers. Moreover, the above-average returns of the top quartile of private equity managers seem to be persistently superior.[28] In other words, by developing

28. JPMorgan Asset Management (2009).

specialized skills in less efficient markets, the top private equity firms have avoided regression to the mean.

In the decades before 2005, a private equity deal above $15 billion was rare. In 2006 and 2007, however, private equity did at least ten deals over $15 billion.[29] Those megadeals were possible because the private equity funds had raised large amounts of cash and were able to borrow even larger amounts on very favorable terms.

Most of the megadeals fared poorly during the financial crisis. Furthermore, from mid-2008 through the end of 2009, the largest private equity funds were not able to invest much of their capital intelligently; the ten largest private equity firms each had more than $10 billion in "dry powder" as of June 2010.[30] Only during the first half of 2010 did private equity firms start to acquire new companies again, and they raised over $9 billion in IPOs to exit from old deals.[31]

As both sides of the private equity market began to pick up, institutional investors were prepared to provide more capital to seasoned managers. But large investors formed the Institutional Limited Partners Association (ILPA), which issued a set of best practices for managers of private equity funds to follow. Those practices called for greater transparency, lower fees, and more generous profit sharing. As a result, the annual management fees and special "deal fees" charged by private equity managers have started to decline.[32] Hurdle rates—the return rates above which incentive fees may be collected by private equity managers—also have become more common. From 2000 to 2002, 73 percent of funds worth at least $1 billion had a hurdle rate, but that percentage rose to 94 percent among funds raised in 2009 and 2010.[33] In short, institutional allocations to hedge funds and private equity funds are rising significantly, while the fees paid by institutional clients of these funds are falling modestly.

Asset Allocation Trends by Type of Institutional Investor

While the three trends in asset allocation after the financial crisis applied generally to all financial institutions, there was significant variation among different types of institutional investors. Here we discuss the asset allocation trends for corporate pension plans, public pension plans, and endowments of foundations

29. Lattman (2010).
30. Creswell (2010).
31. Heath (2010).
32. *Economist* (2010).
33. Jannarone (2010).

and universities. This discussion focuses on asset allocation trends for these types of institutional investors in the United States because of limitations on the ready availability of data for other countries.

Corporate Pension Plans

At the end of 2009, DB plans of U.S. corporations held approximately $2.1 trillion in assets, according to estimates by Cerulli Associates.[34] Most of those plans were established years ago by large U.S. corporations. Due to increasing strict accounting and regulatory rules for DB plans, there are almost no new DB plans in the United States; many existing DB plans have been frozen and closed to new entrants. Most U.S. corporations have come instead to rely heavily on DC plans for their retirement programs.

A look at DB plans in the companies in the S&P 500 Index shows that their funding status was heavily affected by the rise and fall of stock markets before, during, and after the financial crisis. Their funding status was also adversely affected by the decline in U.S. interest rates from the fall of 2008 through 2010, leading to lower discount rates. At the end of 2007, those plans were funded at 107 percent of their required amounts. Their funding status fell to 79 percent at the end of 2008 as the stock market crashed and rose to 82 percent at the end of 2009 because of the stock market rally that year.[35]

Moreover, the percentages in 2008 and 2009 are significantly overstated because many companies have not yet recognized losses from those two years in accordance with the smoothing rules of FAS 87. Under the Pension Act of 2006, new funding rules would have required plans to make contributions to amortize unfunded liabilities over seven years.[36] In response to the financial crisis, however, Congress in 2010 provided relief to DB plans by allowing them to use a fifteen-year amortization schedule or, alternatively, to pay interest for only two years while using a seven-year amortization schedule. Both the fifteen-year schedule and the two years of interest payments would be available for underfunding in two out of four plan years from 2008 through 2011. If a fifteen-year amortization schedule were used by all S&P 500 companies with DB plans, their funding obligations would decline in 2011 from $56 billion to $48 billion. If the two years of interest plus seven-year amortization schedule were used by those companies, their funding obligations would decline in 2011 from $56 billion to $43 billion.[37]

34. Cerulli Associates, telephone interview. Based on data from U.S. Department of Labor, Federal Reserve, EBRI, Federal Thrift Savings Annual Reports, and Cerulli Associates, August 2010.

35. Moran and Cohen (2010).

36. Ingui (2006).

37. Zion, Varshney, and Cornett (2010a).

Thus, even with congressional relief, most DB plans in the United States have substantial funding deficits that will have to be met over the next ten to fifteen years. In general, DB plans will face substantial challenges in closing their long-term funding deficits. By shifting asset allocations from equities to fixed income with lower expected returns, they may make those challenges even tougher. According to an analysis by Goldman Sachs, equity allocation dropped from 56 percent in 2007 to 48 percent in 2009; over the same period, the fixed income allocation rose from 32 percent to 35 percent.[38]

The shift from equities to fixed income seems inconsistent with the return assumptions of most DB corporate plans, which have stayed stubbornly close to 8 percent. Perhaps DB plans expect to reach their return goals by combining lower equity allocations with enhanced exposure to alternative investments, as indicated by an increase from an 8 percent allocation to "other" in 2007 to a 14 percent allocation in 2009.[39] ("Other" in this instance includes any asset class other than equity, debt, and real estate). According to analysis by Credit Suisse, larger DB plans (with over $1 billion in assets) saw the largest drops in equity allocations and relatively high allocations to alternative investments. Conversely, smaller DB plans (with less than $1 billion in assets) have tended to have relatively high allocations to equities and lower allocations to alternative investments.[40] That may be attributable to the relative lack of expertise with alternative investments in small DB plans.

There are other exceptions to the general move of corporate DB plans away from equities and toward fixed income. First, weak corporate DB plans with less than 69 percent funding maintained relatively high allocations to equities and relatively low allocations to fixed income.[41] That may have been an attempt to close the large funding deficit by taking on more year-to-year volatility. Second, some of the largest corporate DB plans in the United States reportedly have delayed a move out of equities and into fixed income because of their interest in converting to liability-driven investment (LDI) and similar strategies. Such strategies are not feasible until a plan becomes at least 90 percent funded.[42] The shift to LDI is a trend that is well under way in the United Kingdom and that DB fund administrators in the United States are seeking to emulate with the goal of extricating themselves from the pension fund management business. (Indeed, the move to close DB plans and shift to DC plans is indicative of the overarching goal of getting out of the DB business altogether.)

38. Moran and Cohen (2010).
39. Moran and Cohen (2010).
40. Zion, Varshney, and Cornett (2010b, pp. 6–9).
41. Zion, Varshney, and Cornett (2010b, pp. 6–9).
42. Haugh (2010).

The general shift from stocks to bonds by corporate DB plans is logical in light of recent events. Having experienced the freezing up of the short-term financing markets for commercial paper and asset-backed securities, many pension managers sought safety by increasing their positions in U.S. Treasuries. It also is possible that mark-to-market accounting will be extended to U.S. pension plans in the near future—perhaps along the lines of the current proposal from the International Accounting Board. The proposed amendments to International Accounting Standard (IAS) 19 would do away with many of the smoothing mechanisms built into current pension accounting. Instead, companies would be forced to recognize changes in the net value of pension obligations through the earnings statement or in "other comprehensive income."[43] In a mark-to-market environment, DB managers would have an incentive to hold more bonds and fewer stocks to reduce the volatility of pension plan returns. Even if stocks earn significantly higher returns than bonds over the long term, the higher volatility of stocks may require a higher level of corporate contributions to a DB plan in any particular year.

Despite the advantages of high allocations to top-quality bonds, they entail significant risks to corporate DB plans. The expected annual return assumptions for U.S. DB plans of S&P 500 companies are now around 8 percent on average.[44] It is hard to see how those returns can be met if DB plans allocated half or more of their assets to fixed income. Moreover, the data suggest that significant purchases of U.S. Treasuries were made at a time when interest rates were historically low. If U.S. interest rates rise over the next five to ten years, DB plans are likely to incur substantial long-term losses on their bond portfolios, which could increase their unfunded deficits. On the other hand, rising interest rates would reduce the size of their overall projected obligations. The net result for any particular plan would depend on a variety of factors, including how well matched the long-term bonds in the portfolio are to the maturity structure of its pension obligations.

Public Pension Plans

At the end of 2009, defined benefit plans of U.S. states and municipalities held approximately $2.7 trillion in assets, according to estimates by Cerulli Associates.[45] Most of those plans were established years ago, and they grew steadily as unions

---

43. Hewitt Associates (2010).

44. Moran and Cohen (2010).

45. Cerulli Associates, telephone interview. Based on data from U.S. Department of Labor, Federal Reserve, EBRI, Federal Thrift Savings Annual Reports, and Cerulli Associates, August 2010.

for public workers bargained for increasing benefits—sometimes in lieu of wage increases. While regulatory and accounting rules for corporate DB plans became much stricter between 1974 and 1999, the rules for public DB plans have only recently become more demanding and still are much less strict than those for corporate DB plans. Similarly, while corporate America has moved dramatically from DB to DC plans, only a few states and municipalities have made the move, though some have supplemented DB plans with some type of DC plan.

As a result, the underfunding of state and local pension DB plans is substantially worse than in corporate DB plans. According to a Pew report entitled "The Trillion Dollar Gap," at the end of fiscal 2008 (ended June 30, 2008), the total pension liabilities of public DB plans in the United States were $2.8 trillion, of which $2.3 trillion was funded, representing an aggregate funding level of 82 percent.[46] But the aggregate funding level obscures the fact that eight states have funding levels below 66 percent. The Pew report clearly understates the funding shortfall in public DB plans because it does not reflect the sharp downturn in the markets during the second half of 2008. For example, Florida, which is one of only two states that thus far has reported 2009 results, realized a return of −18.96 percent for the fiscal year. Florida's funded status dropped from 106 percent funded at the beginning of the 2009 fiscal year to only 93 percent funded at the end of the fiscal year.[47]

Moreover, the funding deficits of public DB plans are understated because of the methodologies that they are allowed to use under Government Accounting Standards Board (GASB) Statement 25, which allows public pension plans to discount future pension liabilities at the same rate that they expect to earn annually on invested assets. In contrast, the Financial Accounting Standards Board requires the discount rate to approximate the rate on high-quality corporate bonds. The Stanford Institute for Economic Policy Research compared the unfunded liabilities of CalPERS and CalSTERS under their expected return assumptions (7.75 percent and 8 percent respectively) to what their liabilities would be if they were using the "risk-free" rate of 4.14 percent for a ten-year U.S. Treasury as their discount rate.[48] The difference was startling—the funding of CalPERS went from 86.1 percent to 49.9 percent, and funding for CalSTERS from 90.9 percent to 50.8 percent.[49] The GASB has resisted efforts to move toward fair valuation of pension assets.

46. Urahn (2010, Executive Summary, p. 1).
47. Florida State Board of Administration (2009).
48. Walsh (2010a).
49. Stanford Institute for Economic Policy Research (2010); Biggs (2010).

While it has proposed in some cases using a discount rate based on high-quality municipal bonds rather than expected returns, that would be applicable only to cash flows needed to eliminate a plan's deficit. Expected returns can still be used as the discount rate for existing plan assets. GASB also would require government plans to amortize some pension costs based on an employee's expected time until retirement, rather than on thirty years of service.[50]

As big as the challenges for public pension plans are, the challenges are much more difficult for public retiree healthcare—referred to as OPEBs (other post-employment benefits). According to the Pew Foundation, the total liabilities for OPEBs were estimated to be $587 billion in fiscal 2008.[51] While other researchers may have somewhat higher or lower estimates, most agree that there is almost no advance funding of OPEBs, as distinct from DB obligations. For example, Pew Research estimated that only about 5 percent of OPEBs were prefunded by states.[52] Because of GASB 45, which is in the process of becoming effective, states and municipalities will have to report publicly on their OPEB liabilities for the first time. However, GASB 45 does not require the prefunding of OPEB liabilities, though it reduces their present value to a significant degree if they will be prefunded in accordance with a definitive plan.

As the pension and OPEB obligations of states and municipalities have risen, their ability to meet those obligations has declined because of the financial crisis. Moreover, many states have opted out of the Social Security system for some of their public employees, such as public school teachers. As a result, states have adopted a variety of measures. In 2010, nine state legislatures approved bills to reduce pension benefits and/or increase pension contributions for current workers. In some states, such as Vermont and Iowa, unions and workers reluctantly supported the changes. In other states, such as Mississippi, the legislature increased the pension contributions of state workers despite their opposition.[53]

Colorado and Minnesota have reduced the annual cost of living increases for the pension benefits of current workers; as a result, both states have been sued for violating state laws.[54] Accrued pension benefits of public employees have constitutional protection in certain states. In the state of Washington, for example, attempts to revise the long-standing method of calculating certain aspects of pension

50. Reilly (2010); Walsh (2010b).
51. Urahn (2010, p. 5).
52. Urahn (2010, p. 5).
53. Neumann (2010b).
54. Neumann (2010a).

benefits for state employees were struck down as violating the state constitution.[55] By contrast, there generally are no constitutional barriers to reductions in OPEBs. But the reductions in OPEBs may be subject to a legal duty or political pressure to bargain with unions representing state employees.

Given the dire situation faced by many states, it is not surprising to see that public DB plans are increasing the expected returns on their investment portfolios to very aggressive levels. For instance, municipal pension funds said that they expect their investment portfolios to beat relevant benchmarks by 160 basis points (bps) in 2009, up from 132 bps in 2008. Public funds with assets of $500 million or less increased their expected outperformance even higher, to 180 bps in 2009, up from 135 bps in 2008. Although public plans with assets between $500 billion and $1 trillion actually decreased their alpha projections from 2008 to 2009, they still expect their portfolios to outperform the market by an average of 174 bps annually.[56]

Those higher return targets were reflected in significant changes in asset allocations by public pension plans. Both corporate and public plans in the United States have been reducing their exposure to U.S. equities. Public pension plans have continued to allocate assets to international/global stocks, in contrast to corporate plans, in which the allocation to this asset category is declining on an absolute basis. On an overall basis, however, corporate DB plans are raising allocations to fixed income in order to de-risk their portfolios. By contrast, public DB plans are cutting their allocations to fixed income.[57]

To which asset classes besides international stocks are public DB plans increasing their allocations? They are adding to alternative investments, such as private equity and hedge funds. According to Greenwich Associates, 23 percent of public funds plan to make significant additions to private equity from 2010 to 2012, and 18 percent plan to significantly increase their allocations to hedge funds during that same period.[58]

This big plunge into alternative investments by public pension plans is understandable. Their executives may be "going for broke" to avoid legislative pressure to increase worker contributions or cut back their benefits. However, as discussed earlier in the chapter, alternative investments do not consistently produce positive returns, and they decreased in value significantly during the financial

55. *Washington Federation of State Employees* v. *State,* 98 Wn.2d 677, 658 P.2d 634 (1983).

56. Greenwich Associates (2010e).

57. Greenwich Associates (2010e).

58. Greenwich Associates (2010e).

crisis. Moreover, we believe that it is important to select a top-quartile fund in certain alternative investments, such as private equity funds, in order to achieve strong results.

Endowments and Foundations

At fiscal 2009 year end, endowment assets in the United States totaled $321 billion and foundations assets were $583 billion, according to estimates by Cerulli Associates.[59] Over the past few decades, the asset allocation policy that endowments and foundations have pursued has been substantially different from that of public and private pension funds. Although all are similar with respect to the fact that their obligations are long term, endowments and foundations have long demonstrated a greater commitment to investing in more esoteric, less liquid options than traditional stocks and bonds. For example, according to data from Cambridge Associates, at the end of fiscal 2009, the college and university mean equal weighted allocation to equities was approximately 36 percent; to fixed income, 14.5 percent; and to cash, less than 5 percent. The remaining 45 percent was invested in hedge funds, distressed securities, private equity, real estate, commodities, and other alternative asset classes.

The asset allocation structure for endowments and foundations has probably been best exemplified by Yale University under the leadership of David Swenson. Yale's average annual return for the decade ended June 30, 2008, was 16.3 percent.[60] Many endowments emulated the Yale model in an attempt to obtain high returns over long periods of time. Yale historically has allocated a significant portion of its portfolio to alternative assets, including hedge funds and private equity. Figure 5-24 includes Yale's target portfolio at the end of its fiscal 2009.

As was the case for all investors, 2008 was a challenging year for endowments and foundations. But it may have been worse for university and college endowments as the confluence of three negative factors created an extremely difficult environment. First, endowments dropped substantially with the decline in global markets. According to a 2009 National Association of College and University Business Offices (NACUBO)–Commonfund study, the average endowment return was −18.7 percent for fiscal 2009.[61] Second, student need rose as the weak economy impacted families' ability to pay tuition. The third blow to endowments

---

59. Cerulli Associates, telephone interview. Based on data from the Foundation Center, NACUBO, and Cerulli Associates, August 2010.

60. Fabrikant (2010).

61. National Association of College and University Business Officers (2010).

Figure 5-24. *Yale University Target Portfolio, June 30, 2009*

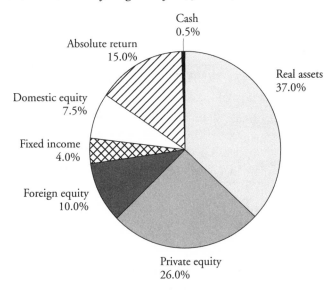

Source: Yale University (www.yaleuniversity.edu/investments).

was a significant fall-off in fundraising. Sixty percent of survey respondents reported a decline in gifts, while only 26 percent reported an increase. Among those who reported a decline, the median decrease was 45.7 percent.[62]

The impact of those events has been profound. Some universities, which had been under political pressure to increase their spending during the good times, moved from offering loans to students to offering them scholarships, thus committing to a higher level of spending. And increasing tuition for full-paying students has not proved to be an alternative to raising funds. Although annual tuition increases have long been above the inflation rate, many private colleges and universities report that with tuition, room, and board exceeding $50,000 annually, their ability to put through further price increases above the inflation rate is limited. To handle higher student need and the ongoing expenses of the operating budget, 43 percent of universities/colleges in the study reported that they increased their spending rate, despite the significant drop in endowment value. Fifty-four percent of those surveyed increased their spending in dollar terms.

62. National Association of College and University Business Officers (2010).

Colleges and universities also resorted to higher debt. Average debt for the participants in the study rose from $109.1 million on June 30, 2008, to $167.8 million on June 30, 2009.[63]

Yale and Harvard, both early adopters of a model that relies heavily on alternatives, announced spending cuts to try to compensate for weak endowment returns (Yale, −24.6 percent, and Harvard, −27.3 percent, in fiscal year 2009). Those measures included employee layoffs, salary freezes, reducing the number of graduate students, reducing support for research programs, and delaying major construction projects.[64] Commitments to private equity also were challenged. The especially illiquid nature of the endowment pools meant that many colleges had trouble meeting their prior commitments to private equity funds, which typically line up commitments for investment some period of time before actually deploying the funds. In some cases commitments were renegotiated and in other cases repudiated.

Despite the pitfalls of a highly illiquid portfolio, endowments seem not to have altered their asset allocation model. Indeed, Yale announced in September 2009 that it was increasing exposure to alternatives. The university increased its allocation to private equity from 21 percent to 26 percent and its target holdings of real estate and commodities from 29 percent to 37 percent.[65]

Data from Cambridge Associates show that the exposure to hedge funds of college and university endowments changed little between June 2008 and June 2009 (14.7 percent and 14.1 percent respectively). Similarly, the average exposure to other alternative strategies (including private equity, real estate, venture capital, arbitrage, distressed securities, and commodities) in aggregate rose modestly, to 44.8 percent from 43.9 percent. At the same time, colleges and universities have continued to reduce their exposure to equities, especially U.S. equities. The fixed-income allocation rose during this time period from 12.3 percent to 14.5 percent. Cash also increased, from a mean allocation of 1.8 percent to 4.8 percent for colleges and universities, according to Cambridge Associates analysis.[66] NACUBO studies also point to relatively high cash levels, which stood at 4 percent for colleges and universities as of June 30, 2009.[67] Higher cash levels make sense given the continued commitment to illiquid asset classes and cash flow difficulties that

63. National Association of College and University Business Officers (2010).

64. Foderaro (2010); *Harvard Magazine* (2009).

65. "2009: The Yale Endowment" (www.yale.edu/investments/Yale_Endowment_09.pdf).

66. Cambridge Associates. Equal-weighted mean allocations based on data from Cambridge Associates, August 2010.

67. National Association of College and University Business Officers (2010).

ensued thereafter; however, with returns hovering around zero, higher cash levels will be a drag on performance.

Foundations also fared poorly during the market decline, with an average return in 2008 of −26 percent, according to a Commonfund study. Although returns rebounded by about 21 percent in 2009, according to John S. Griswold, "returns in the 21 percent range were not enough to move trailing three-year returns into positive territory, and five-year returns in the upper 3 percent range are well short of covering these nonprofit organizations' spending, inflation, and costs."[68]

Independent and private foundations generally do not participate in fundraising, so they have little ability to recoup investment losses by other means. Under U.S. law, they must give away on average 5 percent of their assets over a series of years. Foundations responded to the financial crisis by cutting costs, including administrative expenses, and reducing disbursements. A Council on Foundations survey (March 2009) reported that 60 percent of those who responded to the survey said that they planned to cut operating budgets and 45 percent indicated that they would freeze salaries. In addition, according to the survey, 48 percent of foundations said that they planned to reduce the total value of the grants that they awarded by 10 percent or more in 2009.[69] That, of course, came on the heels of an especially challenging time for many of the beneficiaries of foundation grants.

Nevertheless, like endowments, foundations do not show many changes with respect to their asset allocation policies. Between 2008 and 2009, foundation allocations showed little change, with continued high commitment to alternative assets. However, cash positions rose, with foundations over $1 billion reporting an increase from 2.5 percent in 2008 to 4.7 percent in 2009.[70] Higher cash levels may represent a partial buffer to illiquid assets in the portfolio.

One trend apparent in the data for endowments and foundations that parallels a trend in corporate DB plans is the tendency for larger plans to have more exposure to alternative asset classes and correspondingly less exposure to traditional asset classes. Table 5-7 provides information about exposure to several key asset classes for endowments and foundations over and under $1 billion in 2009. While endowments under $1 billion had nearly 21 percent exposure to U.S. equities, their larger counterparts had only 14.1 percent. Conversely, exposure to hedge funds was 16 percent for larger but 12 percent for smaller endowments. Foundations

68. *Commonfund News* (2010).

69. Council on Foundations (2009).

70. Cambridge Associates. Equal-weighted mean allocations based on data from Cambridge Associates, August 2010.

Table 5-7. *Endowments and Foundations, Asset Allocation for Key Categories, June 30, 2009*

Percent

Asset category	Endowments under $1 billion	Endowments over $1 billion	Foundations under $1 billion	Foundations over $1 billion
U.S. equities	20.9	14.1	22.4	18.8
Global ex U.S. equities	14.4	9.9	15.5	10.6
U.S. bonds	16.1	8.4	15.9	9.1
Hedge funds	12.1	15.9	10.2	12.7

Source: Cambridge Associates. Equal-weighted mean allocations based on data from Cambridge Associates, August 2010.

display a similar pattern. Presumably, the greater reliance on traditional asset classes for the smaller endowments and foundations is related to the lower level of resources and expertise of the in-house staff that monitors and assesses non-traditional asset classes.

Given the difficulties encountered during 2008 to 2009 with the Yale model, it is surprising that the appetite of endowments and foundations for alternatives continues to remain hearty. In a survey conducted by Greenwich of both foundations and endowments in 2009, respondents indicated a clear interest in increasing their exposure to alternatives over the next three years. Over 20 percent of those surveyed said that they would significantly increase their exposure to hedge funds, while only 8.5 percent said that they would significantly decrease their exposure. Similarly, 22 percent intended to significantly increase while only 7 percent intended to significantly decrease their exposure to private equity. Finally, 20.3 percent noted their intention to significantly increase exposure to real estate, while only 3.3 percent would significantly decrease it. The source of funds for the increased allocations to alternative investments is likely to be U.S. equity and fixed-income investments.[71]

Conclusions

The financial crisis of 2008 to 2009 involved the largest upheaval in the securities markets since the Great Depression, in the 1930s. After this crisis, institutional investors changed their asset allocations—both actively, by shifting monies

71. Greenwich Associates (2009).

among asset categories, and passively, by not fully rebalancing their portfolios. Given the severity of the recent financial crisis, it is notable that those changes in asset allocation did not represent radical breaks with the past by most institutional investors. Instead, the changes accelerated three trends that had been gradually building momentum over the past few years.

The first trend is a general decrease in the institutional allocations to equities, with international equities becoming a larger part of the overall equity allocation as the allocation to international equities declines less rapidly than the allocation to domestic equities or, in some cases, actually rises relative to historical levels. That represents a continuing trend among institutional investors away from home country bias and toward better geographic diversification. Although equity markets around the world converged during the height of the financial crisis, they already have decoupled to a substantial extent. The increased exposure to international equities may represent a rising recognition that attractive investment opportunities may exist outside one's home country in developed or emerging market countries.

By contrast, the merits of the general decrease in equity allocations in favor of fixed income—the second major trend noted in this chapter—are more debatable. The increase in fixed income allocations appears to be concentrated primarily in government securities and investment-grade bonds, though it may also include high-yield bonds and emerging market bonds for specific institutions. The shift from equities to high-quality bonds is quite understandable, since such bonds were one of the few asset categories with high returns and good liquidity during the financial crisis. In addition, the shift reflects the nascent concerns about year-to-year volatility of equity returns among pension sponsors, who fear that they will be forced to make up for any unrealized losses in pension portfolios marked to market on an annual basis.

Yet a significant shift from all types of stocks to high-quality bonds seems inconsistent with the expected return of 8 percent a year assumed by most corporate pension plans. Increasing allocations to high-quality bonds in the current environment of very low interest rates also exposes corporate pension plans to considerable interest rate risk. Long-term government and investment-grade bonds acquired in 2009 or 2010 will show large unrealized losses over the next decade if and when interest rates rise. In a rising rate environment, however, those losses may be offset to some degree by a reduction in the overall benefit obligation of corporate DB plans.

Faced with huge funding challenges, public pension plans in the United States have allocated assets from equities to alternative investments rather than to high-quality bonds. However, hedge funds and private equity funds showed substantially negative returns during the financial crisis, despite their implied promises of positive returns in all market environments. While alternative investments have been less volatile than equities over the past few years, they have been more volatile than high-quality bonds. Public pension plans will need to ensure that they have the expertise and resources to find and access the best-performing alternative funds.

Endowments and foundations now also have relatively high allocations to alternative investments. But those allocations were made years before the financial crisis, as many endowments and foundations followed the Yale model of diversifying into nontraditional investment categories. For the same reason, many endowments and foundations decreased their allocations to publicly traded equities and bonds several years before the financial crisis. Although the portfolios of Yale and other large endowments fared poorly during the financial crisis, there seems to be little inclination to reject the Yale model—with the exception of maintaining higher cash levels to deal with funding commitments if another financial crisis should arise.

A heavy allocation to alternative investments is not characteristic of just public pensions and endowments in the United States. The trend toward more alternative investments seems prevalent for all types of institutional investors in most parts of the world. This trend is based on hopes that alternative investments will yield higher returns, with less volatility and better diversification, than traditional holdings in publicly traded stocks and bonds. However, it is by no means certain that institutional investors will be able to accomplish those objectives.

The lower fees charged by alternative funds would certainly help investors' returns. But more important than fees to achieving expected returns is accessing funds of top-performing managers. In contrast to the children in Lake Wobegon, not all alternative managers are above average.[72] Going forward, delivering strong risk-adjusted returns probably will be more challenging, even for alternative managers that had top returns in the past. The ability of managers to deliver strong returns depends on their ability to find and take advantage of market inefficiencies. However, the generation of new opportunities is unlikely to keep up with the flood of new money pouring into the alternatives arena. There is a reasonable likelihood, therefore, that the increased allocations to alternatives may not meet the high expectations of many institutional investors.

---

72. Garrison Keillor popularized the mythical "Lake Wobegon" in his weekly public radio variety show, *A Prairie Home Companion.* In Lake Wobegon, Keillor said, "All the women are strong, all the men are good looking, and all the children are above average."

References

Anson, Mark. 2004. "Strategic versus Tactical Asset Allocation." *Journal of Portfolio Management* (Winter 2004), pp. 8–22.

Biggs, Andrew. 2010. "Public Pension Deficits Are Worse than You Think." *Wall Street Journal,* March 22.

Black, Fischer. 1980. "The Tax Consequences of Long-Run Pension Policy." *Financial Analysts Journal* 36, no. 4, pp. 21–28.

Board of Governors of the Federal Reserve System. 2010. "Flow of Funds Accounts of the United States. Flows and Outstandings. First Quarter 2010." Tables L.118.b, Private Pension Funds: Defined Benefit Plans; L.118.c, Private Pension Funds: Defined Contribution Plans; L.119, State and Local Government Employee Retirement Funds; and L.120, Federal Government Retirement Funds.

Brinson, Gary P., Randolf L. Hood, and Gilbert L. Beebower. 1986. "Determinants of Portfolio Performance." *Financial Analysts Journal* 42, no. 4 (July–August), pp. 39–44.

Brinson, Gary P., Brian D. Singer, and Gilbert L. Beebower. 1991. "Determinants of Portfolio Performance II: An Update." *Financial Analysts Journal* 47, no. 3 (May-June), pp. 40–48.

Brown, Stephen J., William N. Goetzmann, and Roger G. Ibbotson. 1999. "Offshore Hedge Funds: Survival and Performance, 1989–95." *Journal of Business* 72, no. 1 (January), pp. 91–117.

Casey, Quirk, & Associates. 2010. "eVestment Alliance Quarterly Global Asset and Flows Review: First Quarter 2010." Available to subscribers at www.evestmentalliance.com.

Casey, Quirk, & Associates. 2009. "eVestment Alliance Quarterly Global Asset and Flows Review: Fourth Quarter 2009." Available to subscribers at www.evestmentalliance.com.

Commonfund News. 2010. "Foundation and Operating Charity Investment Returns Rise in the Range of 21 Percent in Fiscal Year 2009." Press release, July 1 (www.commonfund.org/InvestorResources/CommonfundNews/Pages/FoundationandOperatingCharityInvestment Returns.aspx).

Council on Foundations. 2009. "Foundations Respond to the Needs of Families Even as Their Assets Have Declined." Survey, March.

Creswell, Julie. 2010. "On Wall Street, So Much Cash, So Little Time." *New York Times,* June 24.

De Sa'Pinto, Martin. 2010. "Alternative Funds Adapt as Fee Pressure Weighs." March 5 (www.reuters.com/article/idUSTRE62431G20100305).

Economist. 2010. "Private Inequity." May 8.

Fabrikant, Geraldine. 2010. "Harvard and Yale Report Losses in Endowments." *New York Times,* September 11.

Florida State Board of Administration. 2009. "Florida State Pension Plan Funding Ratio Projected at 93 Percent." Press release, August 5.

Foderaro, Lisa W. "Yale, with $150 Million Deficit, Plans Staff and Research Cuts." *New York Times,* February 4.

Fung, William, and David A. Hsieh. 2000. "Performance Characteristics of Hedge Funds and CTA Funds: Natural versus Spurious Biases." *Journal of Financial and Quantitative Analysis* 35, no. 3, pp. 291–307.

Greenwich Associates. 2009. "U.S. Investment Management Trends." Proprietary subscriber commissioned survey data. Used with permission.

———. 2010a. "Funds Planning to Increase or Decrease Allocations." Proprietary subscriber commissioned survey data. Used with permission.

———. 2010b. "Asian Investment Management Trends." Proprietary subscriber commissioned survey data. Used with permission.

———. 2010c. "European Investment Management Trends." Proprietary subscriber commissioned survey data. Used with permission.

———. 2010d. "U.K. Investment Management Trends." Proprietary subscriber commissioned survey data. Used with permission.

———. 2010e. "U.S. Corporate Pension Funds Shed Risk, While Public Funds Embrace It." Greenwich U.S. Investment Management Research Report, March (www.greenwich.com).

Harvard Magazine. 2009. "$11 Billion Less." November-December.

Haugh, John. 2010. "Corporate Pensions: Trigger Happy." Bank of America–Merrill Lynch Research Report, March 18.

Heath, Thomas. 2010. "Private-Equity Business Picking Up." *Washington Post,* June 7.

Hewitt Associates. 2010. "Global Report: Proposed Amendments to IAS 19," May.

Ingui, Silvio. 2006. "Pension Protection Act of 2006: United States." Milliman Insight Research Report, October 1.

Institutional Investor Institute. 2010. "European Pension Fund Investment Trends." Survey.

Jannarone, John. 2010. "No Free Ride at KKR despite Push." *Wall Street Journal,* August 8.

JPMorgan Asset Management. 2009. "Private Equity: Exploring the Full Equity Spectrum." November.

Kaplan, Steven N., and Antoinette Schoar. 2005. "Private Equity Performance: Returns, Persistence, and Capital Flows." *Journal of Finance* 60, no. 4, pp. 1791–1823.

Lattman, Peter. 2010. "Buyout-Boom Winners Are Few and Far Between." *Wall Street Journal,* May 18.

Malkiel, Burton G., and Atanu Saha. 2005. "Hedge Funds: Risk and Return." *Financial Analysts Journal* 61, no. 6 (November-December), pp. 80–88.

Moran, Michael, and Abby J. Cohen. 2010. "Pension Review 2010: Pension Palpitations Refuse to Dissipate for Corporate Plan Sponsors." Goldman Sachs Global Markets Institute Research Report, June 11.

National Association of College and University Business Officers. 2010. "2009 NACUBO-Commonfund Study of Endowments." Press release, January 28 (www.nacubo.org).

Neumann, Jeannette. 2010a. "Pension Cuts Face Test in Colorado." *Wall Street Journal,* June 12.

———. 2010b. "State Workers, Long Resistant, Accept Cuts in Pension Benefits." *Wall Street Journal,* June 29.

Phalippou, Ludovic, and Oliver Gottschalg. 2005 "The Performance of Private Equity Funds." Paper presented at Thirty-Second Annual Meeting of the European Finance Association, Moscow, August 24–27 (http://papers.ssrn.com/sol3/papers.cfm?abstract_id=473221).

Posthuma, Nolke, and Pieter Jelle Van der Sluis. 2003. "A Reality Check on Hedge Funds Returns." Free University of Amsterdam Faculty of Economics and Business Administration Research Memorandum, vol. 17, pp. 1–40.

Reilly, David. 2010. "Pension Bombs Need Spotlight." *Wall Street Journal,* June 17.

Stanford Institute for Economic Policy Research. 2010. "Going for Broke: Reforming California's Public Employee Pension Systems." SIEPR Policy Brief, April.

Tepper, Irwin. 1981. "Taxation and Corporate Pension Policy." *Journal of Finance* 36, no. 1 (March), pp. 1–13.

Urahn, Susan. 2010. "The Trillion Dollar Gap: Underfunded State Retirement Systems and the Roads to Reform." Pew Center on the States Research Report, February.

Walsh, Mary W. 2010a. "Analysis of California Pensions Finds Half-Trillion-Dollar Gap." *New York Times,* April 7.

———. 2010b. "A New Plan for Valuing Pensions." *New York Times,* June 24.

Zion, David, Amit Varshney, and Christopher Cornett. 2010a. "Pension Funding Relief, Again." Credit Suisse Research Report, March 10.

———. 2010b. "Pension Asset Allocations: They Are A-Changin.'" Credit Suisse Research Report, May 4.

Contributors

Yasuyuki Fuchita
*Nomura Institute of Capital
    Markets Research*

Richard J. Herring
University of Pennsylvania

Robert E. Litan
*Kauffman Foundation and
    Brookings Institution*

Olivia S. Mitchell
University of Pennsylvania

Akiko Nomura
*Nomura Institute of Capital
    Markets Research*

Robert Novy-Marx
University of Rochester

Betsy Palmer
MFS Investment Management

Robert C. Pozen
MFS Investment Management

Joshua Rauh
Northwestern University

Natalie Shapiro
MFS Investment Management

Index

ABO. *See* Accumulated benefit obligation

Accounting standards: corporate, 53, 56; for defined benefit plans, 2, 128; international, 40, 128; for state and local governments, 47, 129–30. *See also* Liabilities

Accumulated benefit obligation (ABO), 52–53, 57, 62, 63, 64

Adequacy of pension plans, 13, 19–20, 22

Alternative investments: asset allocations by institutional investors, 33, 45, 108–13, 120–25, 127, 131–32, 134, 135, 136, 137–38; returns, 138. *See also* Hedge funds; Private equity funds

Ambachtsheer, Keith, 37

Annuities, 59, 84, 88–89

Argentina, pension funds, 86

Asia: asset allocations by institutional investors, 33, 101, 102, 104, 108, 109, 110, 112; demographic trends, 13–14; shift to private pensions, 19–28. *See also* China; Japan; Korea

Asset allocations: decisions, 35; in defined contribution plans, 42–43, 85, 88; definition, 95; strategic, 95; tactical, 95–96

Asset allocations by institutional investors: alternative investments, 33, 45, 108–13, 120–25, 127, 131–32, 134, 135, 136, 137–38; cash, 134–35; corporate pension plans, 104, 127–28; diversification, 114–18, 137; endowments and foundations, 132, 134–36, 138; equities, 33, 97–104, 114, 118, 127, 131, 132, 134, 137; evaluation of trends, 113–25; fixed income, 33, 104–08, 118–20, 127–28, 131, 132, 134, 137; foundations, 135–36; future intentions, 99, 106–08; by geographic region, 97–113; by investor type, 125–36; performance determined by, 95; policy objectives, 99, 114; public pension plans, 33, 104, 105, 131–32, 137–38; trends, 97–113, 136–37

Automatic enrollment, 27–28, 41, 82, 88

Barclays Treasury indices, 119

Benartzi, Shlomo, 88

Bonds. *See* Fixed-income investments; Government bonds

Boston, public pension funds, 64, 68

Brown, Jeffrey, 64

California, state and local pension plans, 2, 129

Cambridge Associates, 123–24, 132, 134

Canada: asset allocations by institutional investors, 102, 108, 112–13; public pension reserve funds, 30

Canada Pension Plan Investment Board (CPPIB), 33

Casey, Quirk & Associates, 101, 105

Cerulli Associates, 126, 128, 132

Chicago, public pension funds, 50, 64, 68, 72–73

Chicago Teachers' Pension Fund, 50

Chicago Transit Authority, 50

China: corporate pensions, 19, 24, 25, 39, 42, 43; defined contribution plans, 28–29, 39, 42; pension reforms, 11, 28–29, 45; private pension assets, 24; state-owned enterprises, 19

China, public pensions: asset allocation, 29, 33; coverage rates, 22; defined contribution plans, 28–29, 39; description of system, 19; individual accounts, 29; investment policies, 32; partially funded, 29; prefunding, 12, 28–29; replacement rates, 22; reserve funds, 29–30, 35, 36, 43–45

City governments, 50. *See also* Local government pension plans

COLAs. *See* Cost of living adjustments

Commodity investments, 132, 134

Commonfund, 132, 135

COMWEL. *See* Korea Workers' Compensation and Welfare Service

Corporate pension plans: in Asia, 11, 15, 18–19, 24, 25–26, 27, 28, 39–40, 41–43, 45; asset allocations, 104, 127–28; assets, 24, 126; contribution levels, 40–41; coverage rates, 24–25, 26, 27; defined benefit plans, 126–28; in developed economies, 85, 126–28; discount rates used, 56; financial education for employees, 82; government insurance, 85; liability accounting, 53, 56; mandatory enrollment, 25, 38; return assumptions, 128; shift to defined contribution plans, 13, 37–38, 45; unfunded liabilities, 85, 126–27; in United States, 85, 126–28

Cost of living adjustments (COLAs), 52–53, 57, 130

Council on Foundations, 135

County governments, 50, 73. *See also* Local government pension plans

CPPIB. *See* Canada Pension Plan Investment Board

Credit Suisse, 127

DB plans. *See* Defined benefit plans

DC plans. *See* Defined contribution plans

Defined benefit (DB) plans: accounting standards, 2, 128; corporate, 126–28; effects of market shocks, 76–77; in Japan, 18, 26, 39, 40, 45; in Korea, 18, 39; public pensions, 128–29, 131; return estimates, 2; underfunding, 1–2, 129. *See also* Local government pension plans

Defined contribution (DC) plans: advantages, 84, 90; asset allocation, 42–43, 85, 88; automatic enrollment, 27–28, 41, 82, 88; in China, 28–29, 39, 42; company stock in, 88; contribution levels, 40–41; corporate, 13, 37–38, 45; criticism of, 84; effects of market shocks, 76–77; in Europe, 38, 41, 42; 401(k) plans, 38, 41; growth, 38, 77–78; investment decisions, 41–43, 85; in Japan, 24, 26, 39–40, 42–43, 45, 78, 85; in Korea, 39, 41–42, 45; lump-sum cashouts, 88–89, 90; notional, 13; risk management, 88–89; risks, 78–88; shift to, 13, 37–38, 45, 75, 77–78; in United States, 2, 38, 41, 76, 82–84; withdrawals, 82–84, 88–89, 90

Democratic Party of Japan (DPJ), 21

Demographic trends: in Asia, 13–14; fertility rates, 89; life expectancies, 82–84, 88–89; population aging, 1, 12, 13–14

Denmark, defined contribution plans, 38, 41

Developed economies: corporate pensions, 38, 85, 126–28; governance of public pension asset management, 35; pension reforms, 13, 23, 24, 27, 87; private pension assets, 23; private pension coverage rates, 27; public pension reserve funds, 29, 30; replacement rates, 23; returns on pension assets, 76; shift to defined contribution plans, 77–78. *See also* Europe; *and individual countries*

Discount rates: municipal bond yields, 48, 49, 55–56, 62, 63, 130; risk and, 54, 55; Treasury yields, 48, 56–57, 62, 64, 72, 129; used by corporate pension plans, 56; used by local government pension plans, 48–49, 54–55, 129

DPJ. *See* Democratic Party of Japan

EAN. *See* Entry age normal

Earnings fluctuations, 82

EFRP. *See* European Federation for Retirement Provision

Employees' Pension Fund (EPF; Japan), 18, 25–26

Employees' Pension Insurance (EPI; Japan), 15, 20–21, 22, 24

Endowments: asset allocations, 132, 134–35, 136, 138; asset amounts, 132; pressures, 132–34; private equity investments, 118, 134; returns, 132, 134; spending rates, 133; Yale model, 132, 136, 138

Enron, 88

Entry age normal (EAN), 52, 53, 59–60, 62

EPF. *See* Employees' Pension Fund

EPI. *See* Employees' Pension Insurance

Equities: asset allocations by institutional investors, 33, 97–104, 114, 118, 127, 131, 132, 134, 137; domestic, 33, 98,

101, 118; individual exposure, 84–85; initial public offerings, 33, 110, 125; international and global, 101–04, 114, 137; investments in employer's stock, 88; market risk, 85; returns, 114, 119, 137

Eurekahedge, 123

Europe: asset allocations by institutional investors, 101, 102, 104, 106–08; defined contribution plans, 38, 41, 42; pay-as-you-go financing, 19, 29; private pensions, 25; public pension reserve funds, 30, 33; replacement rates, 20, 22–23

European Federation for Retirement Provision (EFRP), 38, 41

FASB. *See* Financial Accounting Standards Board

Federal Reserve Board, 105

Financial Accounting Standards Board (FASB), 53, 56, 129

Financial literacy, 80–82

Financial markets: downturns, 76–77, 135; innovation, 89; liquidity, 118. *See also* Asset allocations; Equities; Returns

Fixed-income investments: asset allocations by institutional investors, 33, 104–08, 118–20, 127–28, 131, 132, 134, 137; domestic, 33, 105, 106; foreign, 33; liquidity, 118; returns, 137; risks, 128. *See also* Government bonds

Florida, public pension funds, 129

Foundations: asset allocations, 135–36, 138; asset amounts, 132; cost-cutting, 135; grants, 135; returns, 135

401(k) plans, 38, 41. *See also* Defined contribution plans

France: public pension reserve funds, 30, 36; shift to defined contribution plans, 38

GASB. *See* Government Accounting Standards Board

Germany, private pension plans, 22–23

Global risks, 87–88

Goldman Sachs, 127–28
Gottschalg, Oliver, 123
Government Accounting Standards Board (GASB), 54; statement 25, 47, 129–30; statement 45, 130
Government bonds: asset allocations by institutional investors, 118, 119, 128, 137; returns, 119, 137; risks, 119. *See also* Fixed-income investments; Treasury securities
Government guarantees, 85–86
Government Pension Investment Fund (GPIF; Japan), 12, 29, 30, 32, 33, 36
Government pensions. *See* Public pensions
GPIF. *See* Government Pension Investment Fund
Greenwich Associates, 104, 106, 109, 131, 136
Griswold, John S., 135

Harvard University endowment, 134
Healthcare for retirees: costs, 86; unfunded liabilities, 130. *See also* Medicare
Hedge funds: asset allocations by institutional investors, 110–12, 120–23, 131, 132, 134, 136; fees, 123; returns, 120–22, 138

See International Accounting Standard
. *See* International Financial Reporting ndards
s, public pension funds, 72, 73
See Institutional Limited Partners ciation
fluctuations, 82
al retirement accounts (IRAs), 18, 27
l risks, 79–85
cost of living adjustments, 52–53,
; effects on pension fund
, 52–53; risk, 57
c offerings (IPOs), 33, 110, 125
Investor Institute, 106–08
investors. *See* Asset allocations
onal investors

Institutional Limited Partners Association (ILPA), 125
Institutional risk, 85–86
Interest rate risk, 120
Interest rates. *See* Discount rates
International Accounting Standard (IAS) *19*, 128
International Financial Reporting Standards (IFRS), 40
Investment policies, 30–33, 34, 36, 99–101, 107–08, 127. *See also* Asset allocations
IPOs. *See* Initial public offerings
IRAs. *See* Individual retirement accounts
Ireland, public pension reserve funds, 30, 33
Italy, shift to defined contribution plans, 38

Japan: accounting standards, 40; asset allocations by institutional investors, 33, 104, 108, 110; corporate pensions, 11, 15, 18, 24, 25–26, 39–40, 42–43, 45; defined benefit plans, 18, 26, 39, 40, 45; defined contribution plans, 24, 26, 39–40, 42–43, 45, 78, 85; equities market, 118; pension reforms, 11, 18, 24, 25–26, 45; population aging, 14; private pension plans, 15, 18, 23–24; savings rate, 43
Japan Association of DC Plan Administrators, 42–43
Japan, public pensions: asset allocation, 33; benefit levels, 21; coverage rates, 22; funding, 20; investment policies, 36; Mutual Aid Pension, 15; prefunding, 12; premiums, 20–21; reforms, 20–21, 22, 37, 45; replacement rates, 21, 23, 26, 27, 45; reserve funds, 29, 30, 35, 36, 37, 43
Jun Kwang-woo, 33

Kaplan, Steven N., 123
Korea: accounting standards, 40; corporate pensions, 18–19, 24, 25, 27, 28, 39, 41–42, 43, 45; defined benefit plans, 18,

39; defined contribution plans, 39, 41–42, 45; Ministry of Employment and Labor, 25; pension reforms, 11, 28, 45; private pension plans, 23–24, 26–27

Korean Life, 33

Korea, public pensions: asset allocation, 33, 45; coverage rates, 22; description of system, 18; investment policies, 32–33; means-tested, 21; prefunding, 12; premiums, 21; reforms, 21, 22; replacement rates, 21, 23, 26–27, 45; reserve funds, 29, 30, 35, 36, 43–45

Korea Workers' Compensation and Welfare Service (COMWEL), 25

Labor, Department of (U.S.), 89

LDI. See Liability-driven investment

Liabilities: accumulated benefit obligation, 52–53, 57, 62, 63, 64; distribution of burden, 73; entry age normal, 52, 53, 59–60, 62; model, 57–62; present value of benefit cash flows, 47–48, 62–64; projected benefit obligation, 52, 53; projected value of benefits, 52, 53, 62, 63, 64; recognition methods, 52–53; simple discounted cash flow formula, 57. See also Discount rates

Liabilities, unfunded: corporate pension plans, 85, 126–27; healthcare for retirees, 130; public pensions, 48–49, 64, 68, 72–73, 85, 129, 130

Liability-driven investment (LDI) strategy, 107–08, 127

Life-cycle problem, 79–80, 82

Life expectancies: increases, 89; outliving, 84, 88–89; uncertainty, 82–84

Life insurance, 33, 84

Local government pension plans: accounting treatment, 47, 129–30; asset allocations, 104, 105, 137–38; average annuities, 59; Comprehensive Annual Financial Reports, 50, 52, 58, 59; default probabilities, 55, 56; discount rates used, 48–49, 54–55,

129; expected returns, 131; liabilities, 52, 62–64, 72–73; liability calculation model, 57–62; participants, 48, 50; present value of benefit cash flows, 62–64; projected cash flows, 59–62, 68; retiree distributions, 59; sample, 48, 50; solvency horizons, 64, 68, 72; unfunded liabilities, 48–49, 64, 68, 72–73, 129. See also Public pensions

Longevity. See Life expectancies

Mark-to-market accounting, 128

Medicare, 86, 87, 89

Mitchell, Olivia S., 82

MSCI World Ex Japan Index, 118

MSCI World Ex US Index, 114, 119

Municipal bond yields, 48, 49, 55–56, 62, 63, 130

Municipalities, 50. See also Local government pension plans

Munnell, Alicia H., 84

National Association of College and University Business Offices (NACUBO), 132, 134

National Employment Savings Trust (NEST; U.K.), 27

National Pension Fund (NPF; Korea), 12, 29, 30, 32–33, 35, 36

National Pension Insurance (NPI; Japan), 15, 20–21

National Social Security Fund (NSSF; China), 12, 29–30, 33, 35, 36

NEST. See National Employment Savings Trust

Netherlands: defined contribution plans, 42; public pension reserve funds, 29

New Jersey, public pension funds, 72

New York City, public pension funds, 64

Norway, Government Pension Fund–Global, 29, 30

Novy-Marx, Robert, 53, 55, 57, 58

NPF. See National Pension Fund

NPI. *See* National Pension Insurance
NSSF. *See* National Social Security Fund

Obama administration, 27
Other post-employment benefits (OPEBs), 130, 131

PBO. *See* Projected benefit obligation
Pension plans: adequacy, 13, 19–20, 22; asset amounts, 29–30, 75–76; coverage rates, 13; effects of market shocks, 76; governance, 32, 34–37; prefunding, 13, 28–37; replacement rates, 20, 21, 22–23, 26–27, 45; sustainability, 13, 19, 45; World Bank conceptual framework, 14–15. *See also* Asset allocations; Corporate pension plans; Defined benefit plans; Defined contribution plans; Liabilities; Public pensions
Pension reforms: automatic enrollment, 27–28, 41, 82, 88; in China, 11, 28–29, 45; demographic trends and, 12; in developed economies, 13, 23, 24, 27, 87; in Japan, 11, 18, 20–21, 22, 24, 25–26, 37, 45; in Korea, 11, 21, 22, 28, 45; trends, 12–14, 43–45
People's Republic of China. *See* China
Pew Foundation, 130
Phalippou, Ludovic, 123
Philadelphia, public pension funds, 68
Political risk, 86, 89
Population. *See* Demographic trends
President's Commission to Strengthen Social Security (*2001*), 87
Private equity funds: asset allocations by institutional investors, 108–10, 120, 131, 132, 136; deal sizes, 125; fees, 125; illiquidity, 110; obligations to, 118, 134; returns, 123–25, 138
Private pensions. *See* Corporate pension plans
Projected benefit obligation (PBO), 52, 53

Projected value of benefits (PVB), 52, 53, 62, 63, 64
Public pensions: accounting standards, 47, 129–30; asset allocations, 104, 105, 131–32, 137–38; asset growth, 128–29; benefit levels, 2; defined benefit plans, 128–29, 131; investment policies, 30–33, 34; pay-as-you-go financing, 12, 13, 15, 19, 29; reserve funds, 29–30, 43–45; reserve management organizations, 33, 34–37; Social Security (U.S.), 86–87, 89, 130; unfunded liabilities, 48–49, 64, 68, 72–73, 85, 129, 130. *See also* Local government pension plans; State government pension plans
PVB. *See* Projected value of benefits

Rauh, Joshua D., 53, 55, 57, 58, 64
Real estate investments, 112–13, 132, 134, 136
Replacement rates, 20, 21, 22–23, 26–27, 45
Republic of Korea. *See* Korea
Retirement planning, financial literacy and, 81–82
Returns: of alternative investments, 138; convergence among asset classes, 114; effects of market shocks, 76; of endowments, 132, 134; of equities, 114, 119, 137; of fixed-income instruments, 119–20, 137; of foundations, 135; of hedge funds, 120–22, 138; negative, 76–77; of private equity investments, 123–25, 138; projections, 131; risk and, 119–20, 128, 137
Risks: in defined contribution plans, 78–88; discount rates and, 54, 55; global, 87–88; individual, 79–85; inflation, 57; institutional, 85–86; interest rate, 120; management, 88–89; national, 86–87; political, 86, 89; returns and, 119–20, 128, 137

S&P *500* Stock Index, 114, 119
St. Paul Teachers' Association Retirement
   Fund, 50
Samsung Life, 33
San Francisco, public pension funds, 64, 68, 72
Savings: encouraging, 88; in Japan, 43
Schoar, Antoinette, 123
Self-employed pensions, in Japan, 15, 18, 39
Singapore, annuities, 89
Social Security (U.S.), 86–87, 89, 130
Solvency horizons, local government
   pension plans, 64, 68, 72
South Korea. *See* Korea
Spain, shift to defined contribution plans, 38
Stakeholder participation bodies, 35–36
Stanford Institute for Economy Policy
   Research, 129
State government pension plans: accounting
   treatment, 47, 129–30; asset allocations,
   104, 105, 137–38; contribution levels,
   72; cost of living adjustments, 57;
   discount rates used, 49; liabilities, 48,
   49, 129; liabilities per household, 72;
   unfunded liabilities, 48, 49, 129, 130.
   See also Public pensions
State Street, 123–24
Stocks. *See* Equities
Sundén, Annika, 84
Sustainability of pension plans, 13, 19, 45
Sweden: defined contribution plans, 38, 41;
   public pension reserve funds, 30, 33;
   public pensions, 19, 29
Swenson, David, 132

Tang, Ning, 88
Target maturity date funds, 82, 88
Tax-qualified pension plans (TQPPs; Japan),
   18, 25, 26

Thaler, Richard, 88
TQPPs. *See* Tax-qualified pension plans
Treasury securities, 105; asset allocations by
   institutional investors, 128; interest rates,
   119–20; returns, 119–20; volatility, 119;
   yields as discount rates, 48, 56–57, 62,
   64, 72, 129
Turner, John, 82

Unfunded liabilities. *See* Liabilities,
   unfunded
United Kingdom: asset allocations by
   institutional investors, 98, 102, 104,
   105, 106–08, 110, 112; defined
   contribution plans, 38, 41; equities
   market, 118; liability-driven investment
   strategy, 127; pension reforms, 23, 27;
   public pensions, 23
United States: asset allocations by
   institutional investors, 97, 98, 101, 102,
   104, 105, 108, 109, 110–12; automatic
   enrollment, 27–28; corporate pension
   plans, 85, 126–28; defined contribution
   plans, 2, 38, 41, 76, 82–84; financial
   literacy surveys, 80–81; pension assets,
   76; Social Security, 86–87, 89, 130. *See
   also* Local government pension plans;
   State government pension plans
University endowments. *See* Endowments

Venture capital. *See* Alternative investments
Venture Economics, 123–24

Wilcox, David, 64
World Bank, 14–15

Yale University endowment, 132, 134, 136,
   138

Brookings Institution

The Brookings Institution is a private nonprofit organization devoted to research, education, and publication on important issues of domestic and foreign policy. Its principal purpose is to bring the highest quality independent research and analysis to bear on current and emerging policy problems. The Institution was founded on December 8, 1927, to merge the activities of the Institute for Government Research, founded in 1916, the Institute of Economics, founded in 1922, and the Robert Brookings Graduate School of Economics and Government, founded in 1924. Interpretations or conclusions in Brookings publications should be understood to be solely those of the authors.

Nomura Foundation

Nomura Foundation is a nonprofit public interest incorporated foundation which aims to address social and economic issues involving Japan and the rest of the world by devoting private sector resources to promote international exchanges and the interchange between social science theory and practice. The foundation also provides grants and scholarships to support the social sciences, arts and culture, and up-and-coming international artistic talent. In the area of World Economy Research Activities it sponsors research, symposiums, and publications on current trends in capital markets of advanced and emerging economies as well as on topical issues in global macroeconomic stability and growth. It relies on a network of institutions from Europe, the United States, and Asia to assist in organizing specific research programs and identifying appropriate expertise.

Nomura Institute of Capital Markets Research

Established in April 2004 as a subsidiary of Nomura Holdings, Nomura Institute of Capital Markets Research (NICMR) offers original, neutral studies of Japanese and Western financial markets and policy proposals aimed at establishing a market-structured financial system in Japan and contributing to the healthy development of capital markets in China and other emerging markets. NICMR disseminates its research among Nomura Group companies and to a wider audience through regular publications in English and Japanese.

Wharton Financial Institutions Center, University of Pennsylvania

The Wharton Financial Institutions Center is one of twenty-five research centers at the Wharton School of the University of Pennsylvania. The Center sponsors and directs primary research on financial institutions and their interface with financial markets. The Center was established in 1992 with funds provided by the Sloan Foundation and was designated as the Sloan Industry Center for Financial Institutions, the first such center designated for a service-sector industry. It is now supported by private research partners, corporate sponsors, and various foundations and nonprofit organizations. The Center has hundreds of affiliated scholars at leading institutions worldwide, and it continues to define the research frontier, hosting an influential working paper series and a variety of academic, industry, and "crossover" conferences.